TAPAS

Tantalizing small plates from the Mediterranean

METRO BOOKS
New York

METRO BOOKS
New York

An Imprint of Sterling Publishing
387 Park Avenue South
New York, NY 10016

ISBN 978-1-4351-3823-0

For information about custom editions, special sales, and
premium and corporate purchases, please
contact Sterling Special Sales at 800-805-5489
or specialsales@sterlingpublishing.com

Manufactured in China

2 4 6 8 10 9 7 5 3 1

www.sterlingpublishing.com

contents

tapas

garlic and paprika char-grilled shrimp

1 pound uncooked large shrimp
1 red bell pepper, coarsely chopped
⅓ cup olive oil
2 cloves garlic, crushed
1 teaspoon smoked paprika
lemon wedges (optional)

1 Shell and devein shrimp, leaving tails intact.
2 Combine shrimp, bell pepper, oil, garlic and paprika in medium bowl.
3 Place on oiled grill pan over medium high heat. Cook bell pepper until browned both sides. Add shrimp towards the end of bell pepper cooking time; cook, turning, until shrimp are changed in color.
4 Serve with lemon wedges, if desired.

prep + cook time 30 minutes **serves** 6

roasted cherry tomato and parmesan dip

1 pint cherry tomatoes
2 teaspoons olive oil
½ cup sour cream
½ cup grated Parmesan cheese
2 tablespoons finely chopped fresh basil
½ teaspoon red pepper flakes
1 loaf sourdough bread, thinly sliced
2 cloves garlic, halved

1 Preheat oven to 425°F (400°F convection).
2 Combine tomatoes and oil on rimmed baking sheet. Roast, uncovered, about 15 minutes or until tomato skins split. Cool 10 minutes.
3 Combine tomatoes, sour cream, cheese, basil and pepper flakes in medium bowl.
4 Toast bread both sides. Rub garlic onto toasts; serve with tomato and parmesan dip.

prep + cook time 35 minutes **serves** 6

shrimp with fresh tomato sauce

1 pound uncooked large shrimp

2 tablespoons olive oil

4 cloves garlic, thinly sliced

4 vine-ripened tomatoes,
   coarsely chopped

2 teaspoons red wine vinegar

1 tablespoon coarsely chopped fresh
   flat-leaf parsley

1 Shell and devein shrimps, leaving tails intact.

2 Heat oil in large skillet; cook garlic until lightly browned. Add tomato; cook, uncovered, stirring occasionally, about 5 minutes. Add shrimp and vinegar; cook until shrimp change color. Stir in parsley.

3 Serve with crusty bread.

prep + cook time 25 minutes **serves** 6

salt cod fritters

1¼ pound salted cod fillet, skin on
3 potatoes (about 1 pound), halved
1 tablespoon olive oil
1 onion, finely chopped
2 cloves garlic, crushed
¼ cup finely chopped fresh flat-leaf parsley
½ cup pitted green olives, finely chopped
1 egg
vegetable oil, for deep-frying

1 Rinse fish under cold water to remove excess salt. Place fish in large bowl, cover with cold water; refrigerate, covered, overnight, changing the water three or four times. Drain fish; discard water.

2 Place fish in large saucepan, cover with cold water; bring to the boil uncovered. Reduce heat, simmer, covered, 5 minutes. Drain fish, discard water; remove skin and bones then flake fish.

3 Boil, steam or microwave potato until tender; drain. Roughly mash potato in large bowl.

4 Meanwhile, heat olive oil in large frying pan; cook onion and garlic, stirring, until onion softens.

5 Combine fish, onion mixture, parsley, olives and egg with potato; mix well.

6 Roll level tablespoons of fish mixture into balls, place on baking-sheet lined with parchment paper; refrigerate 30 minutes.

7 Heat vegetable oil in deep skillet or wok; deep-fry fritters, in batches, until lightly browned and heated through. Drain on paper towels.

prep + cook time 1 hour 30 minutes (+ refrigeration)
makes 40
Salt cod, also known as salted cod, baccalà, bacalao, is available from Italian, Latin and Portuguese delicatessens and some gourmet grocery stores. It needs to be de-salted and rehydrated before use.

broiled mussels with prosciutto

1 pound small black mussels
2 cups water
4 tablespoons butter, softened
2 ounces thinly sliced prosciutto, finely chopped
1 clove garlic, crushed
2 scallions, finely chopped

1 Scrub mussels; remove beards. Bring the water to a boil in large saucepan. Add the mussels, cover; boil about 3 minutes or until mussels open (discard any that do not).

2 Drain mussels; discard liquid. Break open shells; discard top shell. Loosen mussels from shells with a spoon; return mussels to shells, place in single layer on baking sheet.

3 Preheat broiler.

4 Combine butter, prosciutto, garlic and scallion in small bowl.

5 Divide butter mixture over mussels; broil about 3 minutes or until lightly browned.

prep + cook time 30 minutes serves 4

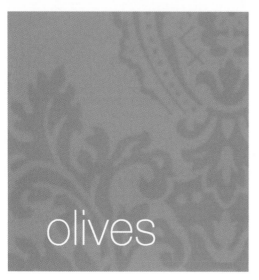

olives

martini olives Rinse and drain
10 ounce jar anchovy-stuffed green
manzanilla olives; combine in medium
bowl with 1 tablespoon finely
chopped fresh rosemary, 4 bay
leaves, 1 tablespoon extra dry
vermouth, 1 tablespoon gin and ½
cup olive oil. Cover, refrigerate
overnight or up to one week. Serve
olives with crusty bread.
prep time 15 minutes (+ refrigeration)
serves 8
*Spanish anchovy-stuffed green
manzanilla olives can be found at
gourmet grocery stores.*

fennel, mint and orange olives
Combine 1 cup pitted ligurian olives,
1 trimmed, thinly sliced baby fennel
bulb, ½ cup fresh mint leaves,
2 tablespoons fresh orange zest,
1 teaspoon black peppercorns and
1½ cups olive oil in medium bowl.
Cover, refrigerate overnight or up to
one week.
prep time 15 minutes (+ refrigeration)
serves 8
*Ligurian olives are medium-sized
black olives found in gourmet grocery
stores; kalamata or any other black
olives can be substituted.*

peri-peri olives Combine 1¼ cups pitted kalamata olives, 1 tablespoon fresh lemon zest, 2 halved fresh small red Thai chiles, 2 garlic cloves, ¼ cup red wine vinegar and ¾ cup olive oil in medium bowl. Cover, refrigerate overnight or up to 1 week.
prep time 15 minutes (+ refrigeration)
serves 8

olives with saffron and cheese Combine 1 cup pimento-stuffed green olives, 2 thinly sliced garlic cloves, 1⅓ cups coarsely chopped semi-hard sheep-milk cheese, ½ teaspoon saffron threads and 1 cup olive oil in medium bowl. Cover, refrigerate overnight or up to 1 week.
prep time 15 minutes (+ refrigeration)
serves 8
Sheep-milk cheese can be found in gourmet grocery stores. substitute other firm cheeses such as Spanish goat cheese, provolone or mozzarella, if desired.

olives with caper berries and sherry vinegar Combine 1¼ cups Sicilian green olives, 1 cup rinsed drained caper berries, 5 sprigs fresh lemon thyme, ¼ cup sherry vinegar and ¾ cup olive oil in medium bowl. Cover, refrigerate overnight or up to 1 week.
prep time 15 minutes (+ refrigeration)
serves 8

pan-seared scallops with anchovy butter

2 teaspoons olive oil
12 large sea scallops (¾ pound)
2 tablespoons butter
3 drained anchovy fillets
2 cloves garlic, crushed
2 teaspoons lemon juice
1 tablespoon finely chopped fresh chives

1 Heat oil in large skillet over medium high heat; cook scallops, both
sides, until lightly browned. Remove from skillet; cover to keep warm.

2 Reduce heat to medium, add butter, anchovies and garlic to skillet; cook, stirring, until garlic is lightly browned. Return scallops to pan with juice; cook until scallops are heated through. Serve scallops drizzled with anchovy butter and sprinkled with chives.

prep + cook time 15 minutes serves 4

saffron and brandy calamari

¼ **pound frozen calamari rings, thawed,
thinly sliced**
2 cloves garlic, crushed
pinch saffron threads
2 teaspoons hot water
1 tablespoon olive oil
2 tablespoons brandy
4 cups baby spinach

1 Combine calamari rings and garlic in medium bowl.
2 Place saffron in small dish; stir in the water.
3 Heat oil in large skillet; cook calamari until lightly browned, remove from pan.
4 Add brandy to skillet; cook about 30 seconds or until brandy has almost evaporated.
5 Add spinach and saffron to pan; cook, stirring, until spinach is wilted. Return calamari to skillet; mix gently. Serve immediately.

prep + cook time 10 minutes **serves** 4

17

chicken, raisin and pine nut empanadas

4 cups water

1 boneless, skinless chicken breast fillet
(about ½ pound)

2 teaspoons olive oil

1 small onion, finely chopped

2 cloves garlic, crushed

¾ cup crushed tomatoes

1 bay leaf

¼ teaspoon red pepper flakes

2 tablespoons raisins, coarsely chopped

2 tablespoons toasted pine nuts

½ teaspoon ground cinnamon

2 tablespoons finely chopped fresh flat-leaf parsley

1 egg

pastry

1⅔ cups all purpose flour

10 tablespoons cold butter, chopped

1 egg

1 tablespoon cold water

1 Bring the water to the boil in medium saucepan;
add chicken, return to the boil. Reduce heat; simmer,
covered, about 10 minutes or until chicken is cooked
through. Cool chicken in poaching liquid 10 minutes.
Remove chicken from pan; discard poaching liquid.
Shred chicken finely.

2 Heat oil in medium frying pan; cook onion and garlic,
stirring, until onion softens. Add undrained tomato, bay
leaf and pepper flakes; cook, stirring occasionally, about
5 minutes or until mixture thickens.

3 Add chicken, raisins, nuts and cinnamon to tomato
mixture; stir until heated through. Stir in parsley. Cool
mixture, covered, in the refrigerator.

4 Meanwhile, make pastry.

5 Preheat oven to 400°F (375°F convection).

6 Roll one pastry half between sheets of baking paper
until ⅛ thick; using 4-inch-round cutter, cut 10 rounds
from pastry.

7 Place 1 level tablespoon of chicken mixture in center of
each round; fold round in half to enclose filling, pinching
edges to seal. Press around edges of empanadas with
a fork. Repeat with remaining pastry half and chicken
mixture to make a total of 20 empanadas, re-rolling
pastry scraps as required.

8 Place empanadas on parchment-lined baking sheets;
brush with egg. Bake 20 minutes or until lightly browned.

pastry Process flour and butter until crumbly. Add egg
and the water; process until mixture comes together.
Knead dough on floured surface until smooth. Divide in
half, enclose in plastic wrap; refrigerate 30 minutes.

prep + cook time 2 hours (+ refrigeration) **makes** 20

potato, dill and shrimp tortilla

2 tablespoons butter
2 teaspoons olive oil
2 medium potatoes (about ¾ pound),
 finely chopped
1 onion, finely chopped
1 pound uncooked large shrimp
6 eggs
2 tablespoons sour cream
2 tablespoons finely chopped fresh dill

1 Preheat oven to 400°F (325°F convection).
2 Heat butter and oil in an ovenproof skillet; cook potato, stirring occasionally, 5 minutes. Add onion; cook, stirring occasionally, until potato is browned and tender.
3 Meanwhile, shell and devein shrimp; add to skillet with potato. Cook until shrimp change color.
4 Whisk eggs with sour cream in bowl until smooth; stir in dill. Pour mixture into pan; stir gently. Cook tortilla over low heat, about 10 minutes or until bottom sets. Place in skillet oven. Cook tortilla, uncovered, about 15 minutes or until tortilla is set and browned.
5 Stand tortilla 10 minutes before cutting into bite size pieces; serve warm.

prep + cook time 45 minutes **serves** 10

sherry-glazed chicken livers

1 tablespoon olive oil
1 pound chicken livers, trimmed, thinly sliced
1 tablespoon butter
2 shallots, finely chopped
⅓ cup dry sherry
½ cup chicken stock
2 small long crusty bread rolls,
   sliced into 6 slices each
1 cup watercress sprigs
1 teaspoon sherry vinegar

1 Heat oil in large skillet; add liver, stir over high heat about 1 minute or until liver is barely cooked. Remove from skillet; cover to keep warm.
2 Add butter and shallot to same skillet; cook, stirring, until shallot softens.
3 Add sherry to skillet; simmer until liquid is reduced by half. Add stock; simmer until liquid is slightly thickened. Return liver to skillet; stir until heated.
4 Toast bread rolls lightly both sides.
5 Spoon liver mixture over toast; sprinkle watercress with vinegar. Top toasts with watercress mixture.

prep + cook time 30 minutes **makes** 12
Chicken filling can be made one day ahead. Pastry can be made one week ahead; keep in the freezer until ready to use.

chorizo and chicken skewers

2 boneless skinless chicken breast (6 ounces each),
cut into 1-inch pieces

2 chorizo (5 ounces each), cut into 1-inch pieces

1 yellow bell pepper,
cut into 1-inch pieces

12 fresh bay leaves

1 tablespoon freshlemon zest

1 tablespoon lemon juice

¼ cup olive oil

2 cloves garlic, crushed

1 teaspoon dried red pepper

¼ cup finely chopped fresh flat-leaf parsley.

1 Combine ingredients in large bowl; cover, refrigerate 30 minutes.

2 Thread chicken, chorizo, bell pepper and bay leaves, alternately, onto skewers.

3 Place on oiled grill pan over medium-high heat. Cook skewers until chicken is cooked through and chorizo is lightly browned.

prep + cook time 30 minutes (+ refrigeration) **makes** 12
Soak 12 bamboo skewers in water for at least an hour before using to prevent them from scorching during cooking.

fennel and garlic roasted pork ribs

1 tablespoon fennel seeds
⅓ cup tomato paste
1 tablespoon brown sugar
¼ cup sherry vinegar
4 cloves garlic, crushed
2 teaspoons smoked paprika
¼ cup olive oil
2 racks pork spare ribs (1 pound each)
lemon wedges (optional)

1 Combine seeds, paste, sugar, vinegar, garlic, paprika and oil in shallow dish, reserving ¼ cup of marinade. Add pork and turn to coat in marinade. Cover; refrigerate 1 hour.
2 Preheat oven to 400°F (375°F convection).
3 Place pork on oiled wire rack over large baking dish; roast, uncovered, 30 minutes.
4 Increase oven temperature to 425°F (400°F convection). Brush pork with reserved marinade; roast about 20 minutes or until cooked through.
5 Slice ribs between the bones; serve with lemon wedges, if desired.

prep + cook time 1 hour (+ refrigeration) **serves** 6

veal meatballs with gazpacho salsa

1 tablespoon olive oil
1 large onion, finely chopped
2 cloves garlic, crushed
1 pound ground veal
2 tablespoons finely chopped fresh oregano
1½ cups grated manchego cheese
1 cup stale breadcrumbs
1 egg
vegetable oil, for shallow-frying
gazpacho salsa
1 cucumber, seeded, finely chopped
1 green bell pepper, finely chopped
½ small red onion, finely chopped
1 small tomato, seeded, finely chopped
2 tablespoons olive oil
1 tablespoon sherry vinegar

1 Make gazpacho salsa.
2 Heat olive oil in medium skillet; cook onion and garlic, stirring, until onion softens. Cool 5 minutes.
3 Combine onion mixture, veal, oregano, cheese, breadcrumbs and egg in large bowl. Roll rounded tablespoons of the veal mixture into balls.
4 Heat vegetable oil in large deep skillet or wok; shallow-fry meatballs, in batches, until cooked through. Drain on paper towels. Serve hot with gazpacho salsa.
gazpacho salsa Combine ingredients in small bowl.

prep + cook time 50 minutes **makes** 40
Manchego cheese is a sharp, firm spanish cheese; it can be found in most gourmet grocery stores. You can use Parmesan cheese instead, if manchego is not available.

fennel and garlic roasted pork ribs

veal meatballs with gazpacho salsa

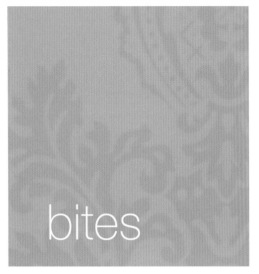

bites

caramelized tomato and ham bites
Cook 2 finely chopped shallots in heated oiled medium skillet until soft. Add 1 pint halved cherry tomatoes; cook 5 minutes. Add ¼ cup balsamic vinegar and 1 tablespoon brown sugar; cook, stirring occasionally, until thickened. Cut 1 brioche loaf into 16 slices; use a biscuit cutter to cut 32 rounds (2 from each slice). Top half the slices with 2 cups finely grated semi-hard sheep-milk cheese; grill until cheese melts. Toast remaining rounds until golden. Divide ⅓ pound thinly sliced double smoked ham among toast rounds; top each with caramelized tomatoes, top with remaining toasts. Serve warm.
prep + cook time 40 minutes **makes** 16

shrimp and caper sandwiches
Combine ½ pound cooked, shelled, finely chopped shrimp, ¼ cup rinsed drained, finely chopped capers, 1 cup mayonnaise, 1 teaspoon sweet paprika, ¼ cup finely chopped fresh flat-leaf parsley and 1 crushed garlic clove in medium bowl. Divide prawn mixture between 9 slices of white bread; top with another 9 slices bread. Trim crusts; cut each sandwich into four triangles.
prep time 30 minutes **makes** 36

asparagus and prosciutto salad bites
Boil, steam or microwave ⅓ pound
trimmed asparagus, drain. Finely
chop asparagus; combine with
1 finely chopped small red onion,
2 tablespoons finely chopped fresh
basil, 2 teaspoons red wine vinegar
and 2 tablespoons olive oil in medium
bowl. Split 10 mini croissants in half.
Divide ⅓ pound thinly sliced
prosciutto among half the croissants;
top with asparagus mixture, then
remaining croissant halves. Serve at
room temperature.
prep time 15 minutes **makes** 10

chicken, almond and tarragon
mini rolls Combine (6 ounces)
cooked finely shredded boneless
skinless chicken breast, ⅓ cup finely
chopped fresh tarragon, ¼ cup
toasted slivered almonds,
1 trimmed finely chopped celery stalk,
3 finely chopped scallions and
⅓ cup mayonnaise in medium bowl.
Make a cut in tops of 12 mini bread
rolls. Spoon chicken mixture into
bread rolls.
prep time 20 minutes **makes** 12
*Chicken mixture can be made one
day ahead; keep, covered, in the
refrigerator.*

blue cheese and fig bites Process
⅓ cup toasted slivered almonds
with 2 coarsely chopped scallions, 1
cup loosely packed fresh mint leaves,
⅓ cup olive oil and
1 tablespoon lemon juice until
smooth. Halve 1 long turkish loaf
lengthways; cut each half lengthways
into 3 fingers then cut fingers into four
crossways to get 24 slices. Toast
bread under broiler. Spread almond
mixture on half the toasts; top with
⅓ pound thinly sliced semi-dried figs
and 4 ounces thinly sliced blue
cheese. Top with remaining toast;
serve warm.
prep + cook time 20 minutes
makes 12

artichoke and asparagus fritters with olive relish

½ pound asparagus, trimmed, finely chopped
1 can (4 ounces) artichokes in brine, drained,
    finely chopped
2 eggs
2 tablespoons finely chopped fresh mint
½ cup grated Parmesan cheese
¼ cup self-rising flour
vegetable oil, for shallow frying
olive relish
½ cup pitted green olives, finely chopped
½ cup pitted black olives, finely chopped
¼ cup finely chopped fresh flat-leaf parsley
1 tablespoon finely chopped fresh chives
1 tablespoon olive oil
1 tablespoon lemon juice

1 Make olive relish.
2 Combine asparagus, artichoke, eggs, mint, cheese and flour in medium bowl.
3 Heat oil in large deep skillet or wok; shallow-fry heaped tablespoons of fritter mixture, in batches, until browned all over and cooked through. Drain fritters on paper towels; serve hot with olive relish.
olive relish Combine ingredients in small bowl.

prep + cook time 40 minutes **makes** 15

roasted eggplant with marjoram vinaigrette

1 large eggplant (about 1 pound), sliced into ½-inch
  rounds
¼ cup olive oil
1 small red onion, thinly sliced
¼ cup sherry vinegar
2 teaspoons sugar
2 tablespoons finely chopped fresh marjoram
½ cup olive oil, extra

1 Preheat oven to 400°F (375°F convection).
2 Brush both sides of eggplant slices with oil; place,
in single layer, on baking-sheets lined with parchment.
Bake about 25 minutes, turning eggplant slices once,
until lightly browned both sides.
3 Meanwhile, combine onion, vinegar, sugar, marjoram
and extra oil in small bowl; spoon over eggplant.
4 Serve warm or at room temperature with crusty bread.

prep + cook time 50 minutes **serves** 6

anchovy and goat cheese baked mushrooms

1 pound portabello mushrooms
1¾ cup (120g) stale breadcrumbs
120g soft goat cheese
¼ cup olive oil
4 drained anchovy fillets, finely chopped
⅓ cup finely chopped fresh chives
1 cup chicken stock

1 Preheat oven to 400°F (375°F convection).
2 Place mushroom caps, in single layer, in medium baking dish.
3 Combine breadcrumbs, cheese, oil, anchovy and chives in medium bowl. Stuff mushrooms with mixture.
4 Add stock to baking dish; bake, uncovered, about 15 minutes or until mushrooms are lightly browned.

prep + cook time 40 minutes makes 20

roasted thyme potatoes with spicy sauce

1 pound baby new potatoes, halved

2 tablespoons olive oil

1 tablespoon finely chopped fresh thyme

spicy sauce

1 tablespoon olive oil

1 small onion, finely chopped

2 cloves garlic, thinly sliced

1 fresh small red thai chile, finely chopped

1 can (15 ounces) crushed tomatoes

2 teaspoons sugar

1 Preheat oven to 425°F (375°F convection).

2 Combine potatoes, oil and thyme in large baking dish; roast about 30 minutes or until potato is tender.

3 Meanwhile, make spicy sauce.

4 Serve spicy sauce with hot roasted potatoes.

spicy sauce Heat oil in medium saucepan; cook onion, garlic and chile, stirring occasionally, until onion is soft. Add undrained tomatoes and sugar; bring to the boil. Reduce heat; simmer, uncovered, stirring occasionally, about 10 minutes or until sauce thickens.

prep + cook time 45 minutes **serves** 8

rosemary potatoes with leek and chorizo

1 pund baby new potatoes, thickly sliced

2 chorizo (5 ounces each), cut into ½-inch thick slices

1 large leek, trimmed, coarsely chopped

6 cloves garlic

1 tablespoon finely chopped fresh rosemary

2 teaspoons sweet paprika

5 bay leaves

¼ cup olive oil

1 Preheat oven to 425°F (400°F convection).

2 Combine ingredients in large baking dish. Roast, uncovered, about 30 minutes or until potatoes are lightly browned.

prep + cook time 45 minutes **serves** 8

braised artichokes with crunchy almond topping

6 large artichokes (about 5 pounds)

½ lemon

4 bay leaves

4 cloves garlic

4 cups chicken stock

crunchy almond topping

¾ cup stale breadcrumbs

⅓ cup sliced almonds

2 tablespoons finely chopped fresh flat-leaf parsley

½ cup pitted green olives, finely chopped

¼ cup olive oil

1 tablespoon fresh lemon zest

2 tablespoons lemon juice

1 Preheat oven to 400°F (375°F convection).

2 Prepare artichokes by snapping off tough outer leaves and peeling stems. Trim stems to about 2 inches. Cut about ¾ inch off top of artichokes to reveal chokes. Cut artichokes in half from top to bottom, then scoop out and discard furry chokes from the centers. As you finish preparing each artichoke, place it in a large bowl of water containing the juice of half a lemon (this stops any discoloration while you are preparing the next one).

3 Drain artichokes. Combine artichokes, bay leaves, garlic and stock in small baking dish, ensuring artichokes are covered with stock. Bake, covered, 45 minutes or until artichokes are tender.

4 Meanwhile, make crunchy almond topping.

5 Drain artichokes; discard liquid.

6 Serve artichokes hot or at room temperature sprinkled with crunchy almond topping.

crunchy almond topping Combine breadcrumbs and nuts on rimmed baking sheet; bake about 5 minutes, cool 5 minutes. Combine breadcrumb mixture with remaining ingredients in small bowl.

prep + cook time 1 hour 40 minutes **serves** 6

smoked eggplant and pepper jam

1 large eggplant, peeled finely chopped
1 medium red bell pepper, finely chopped
1 red onion, finely chopped
¼ cup olive oil
1 tablespoon fresh thyme leaves
1 tablespoon smoked paprika
¼ teaspoon cayenne pepper
¼ cup lemon juice
½ cup water
pita bread

1 Preheat oven to 425°F (400°F convection).
2 Combine eggplant, bell pepper, onion and oil on a rimmed baking sheet with parchment paper; roast, uncovered, about 30 minutes or until vegetables are lightly browned.
3 Combine roasted vegetables, thyme, paprika, pepper, juice and the water in medium saucepan. Bring to the boil; reduce heat, simmer, uncovered, about 10 minutes or until jam is thickened.
4 Serve jam, warm or at room temperature, with char-grilled pita bread.

prep + cook time 1 hour **serves** 8
Smoked eggplant and bell pepper jam can be tossed with pasta, spread on pizza, or served as side dish to chicken, lamb or fish.

pickled quail eggs and beets

12 quail eggs
1 pound baby beets, leaves trimmed
4 cups cider vinegar
¾ cup sugar
2 bay leaves
1 tablespoon black peppercorns
2 teaspoons finely grated fresh horseradish
¼ cup lightly packed fresh dill leaves

1 Sterilize a 5-cup jar and lid.
2 Add eggs to small saucepan of boiling water; simmer, uncovered, about 6 minutes. Drain, then shell eggs.
3 Trim leaves from beets; place unpeeled beets in large saucepan of boiling water. Boil, covered, about 20 minutes or until beets are tender. Cool beets 10 minutes then peel.
4 Combine vinegar, sugar, bay leaves, peppercorns and horseradish in medium saucepan; stir over heat until sugar dissolves then bring to the boil. Remove from heat, stir in dill.
5 Place eggs and beets in hot sterilized jar; pour in enough vinegar mixture to cover eggs and beets. Seal jar; cool. Refrigerate overnight or for up to 1 week.

prep + cook time 1 hour (+ refrigeration) **serves** 6
Wear disposable gloves when handling cooked beets. If you squeeze the warm beets, the skins should burst and peel away easily.
Quail eggs are available from gourmet grocery stores and some farmer's markets. Fresh horseradish is available from most grocery stores.

fava beans and thyme

1 pound frozen fava beans, thawed
2 teaspoons butter
2 shallots, finely chopped
½ pound pancetta, finely chopped
1 tablespoon fresh thyme leaves
1 tablespoon lemon juice

1 Drop beans into medium saucepan of boiling water, return to the boil; drain. When beans are cool enough to handle, peel away gray-colored outer shells.
2 Heat butter in large skillet; cook shallot and pancetta, stirring, until pancetta is lightly browned. Add beans and thyme; cook, stirring, until beans are heated through. Stir in juice.

prep + cook time 40 minutes **serves** 4
Substitute center cut bacon for pancetta if necessary.

chorizo and chickpeas in white wine

1 tablespoon olive oil
1 small onion, finely sliced
2 cloves garlic, crushed
2 chorizo (5 ounces each), coarsely chopped
1 red bell pepper, finely sliced
1 can (15 ounces) chickpeas, rinsed, drained
½ teaspoon smoked paprika
¼ cup dry white wine
⅓ cup chicken stock

1 Heat oil in large skillet; cook onion, garlic and chorizo, stirring, until chorizo is lightly browned.
2 Add bell pepper, chickpeas and paprika; cook, stirring, until bell pepper softens. Add wine and stock; cook, stirring, until liquid is reduced by half.

prep + cook time 25 minutes **serves** 6

fava beans and thyme

chorizo and chickpeas in white wine

antipasto

giardiniera

2 red bell peppers

4 cups white vinegar

2 cups water

6 black peppercorns

1 bay leaf

1 tablespoon sea salt

1 small eggplant (about ½ pound), quartered
lengthways,
cut into ½ inch slices

½ small cauliflower, cut into florets

2 carrots, thinly sliced

2 stalks celery, trimmed, thickly sliced

2 tablespoons finely chopped fresh
flat-leaf parsley

2 teaspoons finely chopped fresh thyme

2 cups olive oil

2 cloves garlic, thinly sliced

1 Preheat oven to 400°F (375°F convection). Sterilize 6-cup jar and lid.

2 Quarter bell peppers; discard seeds and membranes. Roast bell pepper, skin-side up, until skin blisters and blackens. Transfer bell peppers to a glass bowl and cover for 5 minutes; peel away skin then slice thickly.

3 Meanwhile, combine vinegar, the water, peppercorns, bay leaf and half the salt in large saucepan; heat without boiling. Add eggplant, cauliflower, carrot and celery; bring to the boil. Reduce heat; simmer, uncovered, about 5 minutes or until vegetables are tender. Drain vegetables; discard liquid.

4 Combine hot vegetables, bell pepper, herbs and remaining salt in large heatproof bowl. Spoon vegetable mixture into sterilized jar.

5 Heat oil and garlic in small saucepan, strain into large glass measuring cup; discard garlic. Carefully pour hot oil over vegetables in jar to completely cover vegetables, leaving a ½ inch space between vegetables and top of jar. Seal while hot. Refrigerat when cool.

prep + cook time 1 hour **makes** 6 cups

Derived from an Italian word meaning 'garden', giardiniera is an Italian dish of pickled vegetables, often served as part of an antipasto platter. Store in the refrigerator for up to three months. Serve with crusty bread or as part of an antipasto platter with cheeses and deli meats.

roasted fennel dip

4 baby fennel bulbs with fronds (about 1 pound)
2 cloves garlic, unpeeled
1 tablespoon olive oil
1 cup sour cream

1 Preheat oven to 400°F (375°F convection).
2 Halve fennel lengthways; remove and discard cores. Reserve 2 teaspoons coarsely chopped fennel fronds.
3 Combine fennel, garlic and oil in small baking dish; roast, uncovered, about 30 minutes or until fennel is tender. Cool.
4 Peel garlic; blend or process fennel, garlic and sour cream until smooth. Serve dip sprinkled with reserved fennel fronds.

prep + cook time 45 minutes **makes** 1½ cups
serve with garlic pizza wedges, see page 51.

white bean dip

1 tablespoon olive oil
1 leek, thinly sliced
1 can (15 ounces) white beans, rinsed, drained
1 cup heavy cream
1 teaspoon fresh lemon zest
1 tablespoon lemon juice
2 tablespoons finely chopped fresh flat-leaf parsley

prep + cook time 25 minutes **makes** 2½ cups
We used cannellini beans in this recipe but you can use any white bean you like.

1 Heat oil in small skillet; cook leek, stirring, about 10 minutes or until leek softens. Cool.
2 Blend or process leek, beans, cream, zest and juice until smooth. Stir in parsley. Serve with crusty bread.

roasted pepper and walnut dip

2 red bell peppers
8 ounces cream cheese
½ cup finely chopped toasted walnuts

1 Preheat oven to 425°F (400°F convection).
2 Quarter bell peppers; discard seeds and membranes. Roast, skin-side up, until skin blisters and blackens. Transfer to a large glass bowl. Cover for 5 minutes; peel away skin, then chop coarsely.
3 Blend or process bell pepper and cream cheese until smooth; stir in nuts.

prep + cook time 40 minutes **makes** 2 cups
serve with garlic pizza wedges, see page 51.

chunky olive and herb dip

½ cup finely chopped pitted green olives
½ cup finely chopped fresh flat-leaf parsley
½ cup finely chopped fresh mint
¼ cup finely chopped fresh dill
6 drained anchovy fillets, finely chopped
2 teaspoons fresh lemon zest
¼ cup lemon juice
½ cup olive oil

1 Combine ingredients in medium bowl.

prep time 20 minutes **makes** 1½ cups
serve with garlic pizza wedges, see page 51.

garlic pizza wedges

1 cup warm water

1 teaspoon sugar

1 package (¼ ounce) active dry yeast

2½ cups all-purpose flour

1 teaspoon salt

1 tablespoon olive oil

2 cloves garlic, crushed

2 tablespoons grated Parmesan cheese

1 Combine the water, sugar and yeast in glass measuring cup. Stand in warm place about 10 minutes or until frothy.

2 Sift flour and salt into large bowl. Add yeast mixture; mix to a soft dough. Knead dough on floured surface about 10 minutes or until smooth and elastic. Place dough in oiled large bowl; cover. Stand in warm place about 1 hour or until dough is doubled in size.

3 Preheat oven to 425°F (400°F convection). Coat two pizza trays or baking sheets with olive oil.

4 Divide dough in half. Roll each portion into a 12-inch round; place on trays.

5 Brush pizza bases with combined oil and garlic; sprinkle with cheese.

6 Bake pizzas about 20 minutes or until browned and crisp. Cut each pizza into 16 wedges.

prep + cook time 1 hour (+ standing) **makes** 32
This recipe is a good accompaniment for the dips in this book.

stuffed baby bell peppers

24 bell peppers
8 ounces ricotta cheese
2 tablespoons grated Parmesan cheese
2 tablespoons coarsely chopped toasted pine nuts
4 slices hot salami, finely chopped
2 tablespoons finely chopped fresh oregano

1 Preheat oven to 400°F (375°F convection).
2 Carefully cut tops from bell peppers; reserve tops. Scoop out and discard seeds and membranes.
3 Combine remaining ingredients in small bowl. Place mixture in medium piping bag fitted with ½ inch plain tube. Pipe filling into bell peppers; replace tops. Arrange bell peppers, in single layer, in oiled medium shallow baking dish.
4 Roast about 20 minutes or until tender. Serve hot or cold.

prep + cook time 1 hour **makes** 24
You will need about ¾ pound of baby bell peppers for this recipe. Like regular bell peppers, these can be orange, red or yellow and are about the size of jalapeño peppers.

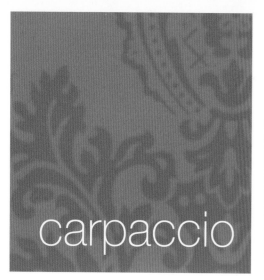

carpaccio

salmon carpaccio Tightly wrap ³/₄ pound piece sashimi salmon in plastic wrap; freeze 1 hour. Unwrap salmon; slice thinly. Arrange slices on serving platter; drizzle with 2 tablespoons white wine vinegar. Refrigerate 1 hour. Slice 2 baby fennel bulbs thinly. Reserve 2 teaspoons finely chopped fennel fronds. Combine fennel, fronds, 2 teaspoons fresh orange zest, ¼ cup orange juice, 1 tablespoon olive oil and 1 teaspoon finely chopped fresh thyme in medium bowl. Drain excess vinegar from salmon; serve topped with fennel mixture.

prep time 30 minutes (+ freezing and refrigeration) **serves** 8

zucchini carpaccio Using vegetable peeler, slice 3 large zucchinis lengthways into ribbons. Combine zucchini in medium bowl with 2 tablespoons olive oil, ¼ cup white wine vinegar, 2 teaspoons sugar, 2 tablespoons finely chopped fresh chives and 1 pitted, finely chopped medium roma tomato.
Cover; refrigerate 30 minutes. Serve zucchini carpaccio sprinkled with 2 tablespoons toasted slivered almonds.

prep time 20 minutes (+ refrigeration) **serves** 8

beef carpaccio Tightly wrap ¾ pound piece beef tenderloin in plastic wrap; freeze 1 hour or until firm. Unwrap beef; slice as thinly as possible. Arrange slices on platter. Combine 2 tablespoons olive oil, 2 teaspoons fresh lemon zest, 2 tablespoons lemon juice, 1 crushed clove garlic, ⅓ cup finely chopped fresh flat-leaf parsley, 2 tablespoons finely chopped fresh oregano and ⅓ cup finely chopped baby arugula in small bowl. Serve beef sprinkled with herb mixture and ⅓ cup flaked Parmesan cheese.
prep time 30 minutes (+ freezing)
serves 8

mackeral carpaccio Tightly wrap ¾ pound piece sashimi mackeral in plastic wrap; freeze 1 hour or until firm. Unwrap fish; slice as thinly as possible. Arrange slices on platter; drizzle fish with ¼ cup lemon juice. Cover; refrigerate 1 hour. Combine 2 tablespoons olive oil, 1 small red onion, thinly sliced, 1 cup loosely packed fresh flat-leaf parsley leaves and 2 tablespoons rinsed, drained baby capers in medium bowl. Drain juice from fish; serve with onion mixture.
prep time 30 minutes (+ freezing and refrigeration) **serves** 8
Use whatever firm white sashimi-type fish you like.

tuna carpaccio Tightly wrap ¾ pound piece sashimi tuna in plastic wrap; freeze 1 hour. Unwrap tuna; slice as thinly as possible. Arrange slices on platter; drizzle tuna with ¼ cup lime juice. Cover; refrigerate 1 hour. Combine 2 tablespoons olive oil, 1 finely chopped fresh long red chile, ¼ cup finely shredded fresh basil and 2 tablespoons coarsely chopped toasted pistachios in medium bowl. Drain juice from tuna; serve tuna with basil mixture.
prep time 30 minutes (+ freezing and refrigeration) **serves** 8

eggplant fritters

2 large eggplants
1 cup grated mozzarella cheese
½ cup coarsely chopped fresh flat-leaf parsley
2 cloves garlic, crushed
½ cup packaged breadcrumbs
¼ cup all-purpose flour
2 eggs
vegetable oil, for shallow-frying
lemon wedges (optional)

1 Preheat oven to 425°F (400°F convection).
2 Remove and discard stem ends from eggplants; prick eggplants all over with fork. Place on oiled baking sheet; roast, uncovered, about 30 minutes or until soft. Cool. Peel eggplants; chop flesh finely.
3 Combine eggplant, cheese, parsley, garlic, breadcrumbs, flour and eggs in large bowl. Using wet hands, shape level tablespoons of mixture into oval patties.
4 Heat oil in large deep skillet or wok; cook fritters, in batches, until browned both sides. Drain on paper towels. Serve fritters warm or cold, with lemon wedges, if desired.

prep + cook time 1 hour **makes** 36

pea and pancetta frittatas

1 teaspoon olive oil
4 slices pancetta (about 2 ounces), finely chopped
1 clove garlic, crushed
6 eggs
⅔ cup light cream
½ cup frozen peas
⅓ cup grated Parmesan cheese
1 tablespoon finely chopped fresh mint
1 teaspoon fresh lemon zest
2 tablespoons crème fraîche
36 small fresh mint leaves

1 Preheat oven to 400°F (375°F convection). Coat three 12-hole (1-tablespoon) mini muffin pans with cooking spray.
2 Heat oil in small skillet; cook pancetta and garlic, stirring, until pancetta is crisp. Cool.
3 Whisk eggs and cream in large bowl; stir in pancetta mixture, peas, cheese, mint and zest. Ladle egg mixture into pan holes.
4 Bake frittatas about 12 minutes or until set. Stand in pan 5 minutes before removing. Serve topped with crème fraîche and mint leaves.

prep + cook time 30 minutes makes 36

ricotta-stuffed prosciutto and melon

smoked trout dip

ricotta-stuffed prosciutto and melon

½ cantaloupe
5 slices prosciutto (about 2 ounces)
⅓ cup ricotta cheese
1 tablespoon finely chopped fresh chives
2 tablespoons finely chopped toasted walnuts

1 Peel cantaloupe; cut lengthways into 10 slices. Cut each slice in half crossways.
2 Cut prosciutto in half lengthways; cut each slice in half crossways.
3 Combine remaining ingredients in small bowl.
4 Spread cheese mixture over one side of each prosciutto; wrap prosciutto firmly around melon.

prep time 20 minutes **makes** 20
You could use halved fresh figs instead of the cantaloupe, if desired.

smoked trout dip

1 potato, coarsely chopped
¼ cup warm milk
1 piece (about 5-6 ounces) smoked trout, flaked
1 clove garlic, crushed
2 tablespoons olive oil
2 scallions, finely chopped
poppy seed crackers

1 Boil, steam or microwave potato until tender; drain. Push potato through fine sieve or potato ricer into small bowl; stir in milk.
2 Combine trout, garlic, oil and onion in medium bowl; fold in potato mixture.
3 Serve dip with poppy seed crackers, if desired.

prep + cook time 30 minutes **makes** 1½ cups

roasted vegetable and mascarpone terrine

1 red bell pepper
1 zucchini, thinly sliced lengthways
2 baby eggplants, thinly sliced lengthways
12 slices prosciutto (6 ounces)
8 ounces mascarpone cheese
2 eggs
¼ cup finely chopped fresh basil

1 Preheat oven to 400°F (375°F convection).
2 Quarter bell peppers; discard seeds and membranes. Transfer bell peppers to a glass bowl. Roast, skin-side up, until skin blisters and blackens. Cover bell pepper for 5 minutes; peel away skin, then chop bell pepper finely.
3 Meanwhile, place on oiled grill pan over medium-high heat; cook zucchini and eggplant, in batches, until tender; cool. Chop vegetables finely.
4 Reduce oven temperature to 350°F (325°F convection). Coat two 3 x 5½ inch loaf pans with cooking spray.
5 Line base and sides of pans with prosciutto, leaving overhang on sides of pans.
6 Combine cheese and eggs in medium bowl; stir in vegetables and basil. Carefully divide mixture between pans and spread evenly; fold prosciutto over to cover. Cover pans tightly with foil; place on baking sheet.
7 Roast 30 minutes. Uncover, roast 30 minutes or until firm. Cool. Refrigerate 3 hours before cutting each pan into 16 slices.

prep + cook time 1 hour 30 minutes (+ refrigeration)
makes 16 slices
Use a traditional terrine pan (3x10 inch) in place of the two smaller loaf pans if your prefer.

cheese and spinach polenta

fried bocconcini with pepper sauce

cheese and spinach polenta

4 cups milk
1 cup polenta
½ cup grated mozzarella cheese
¼ cup grated Parmesan cheese
½ pound finely chopped thawed, drained frozen
   spinach
1 pint cherry tomatoes, halved
1 tablespoon balsamic vinegar
1 tablespoon olive oil

1 Coat a 9-inch cake pan with cooking spray.
2 Bring milk to the boil in medium saucepan; gradually
stir in polenta. Cook, stirring, about 10 minutes or until
polenta thickens. Stir in cheeses and spinach. Spread
polenta mixture into pan, cover; refrigerate 2 hours or
overnight or until firm.
3 Preheat oven to 400°F (375°F convection).
4 Turn polenta onto board; cut into 25 squares. Place
polenta onto baking sheet lined with parchment paper.
Bake about 20 minutes or until lightly browned.
5 Meanwhile, combine tomato, vinegar and oil in small
baking dish. Roast, alongside polenta, about 15 minutes or
until tomato softens slightly.
6 Serve polenta squares topped with tomato halves;
drizzle with tomato pan juices.

prep + cook time 45 minutes (+ refrigeration) **makes** 25

fried bocconcini with pepper sauce

1 red bell pepper
2 roma tomatoes, halved
2 cloves garlic, unpeeled
2 teaspoons olive oil
2 tablespoons all-purpose flour
1 egg, lightly beaten
½ cup packaged breadcrumbs
¼ cup grated Parmesan cheese
2 tablespoons finely chopped fresh
   flat-leaf parsley
2 teaspoons fresh lemon zest
16 cherry bocconcini cheese (8 ounces)
vegetable oil, for deep-frying

1 Preheat oven to 425°F (400°F convection).
2 Quarter bell pepper; remove seeds and membranes.
Combine bell pepper, tomato, garlic and oil in small
baking dish; roast, uncovered, about 20 minutes or until
vegetables soften.
3 Peel garlic; blend or process garlic and vegetable
mixture until smooth.
4 Place flour and egg in separate small shallow bowls.
Combine breadcrumbs, Parmesan, parsley and zest
in another small shallow bowl.
5 Coat bocconcini in flour; shake off excess. Dip in
egg, then in breadcrumb mixture.
6 Meanwhile heat oil in wok; deep-fry bocconcini,
in batches, until golden. Drain on wire rack over tray.
7 Serve bocconcini with roasted pepper sauce.

prep + cook time 1 hour **makes** 16

grilled seafood platter

16 uncooked jumbo shrimp

1 teaspoon fresh lemon zest

½ teaspoon red pepper flakes

1 clove garlic, crushed

1 tablespoon finely chopped fresh oregano

2 tablespoons olive oil

8 slices prosciutto (¼ pound)

8 butterflied sardines (½ pound)

½ pound frozen baby octopus, thawed and
    quartered

½ pound frozen calamari rings, thawed

2 tablespoons balsamic vinegar

¼ cup coarsely chopped fresh flat-leaf parsley

1 pound mussels

½ cup water

¼ cup lemon juice

1 medium tomato (150g), pitted, finely chopped

1 Cut shrimp lengthwise, three-quarters of the way through, (and down to ½ inch before the tail) leaving shells intact; press down on shrimp on cutting board to flatten.

2 Combine shrimp, zest, pepper flakes, garlic, oregano and half the oil in medium bowl; cover, refrigerate 1 hour.

3 Wrap a prosciutto slice firmly around each sardine.

4 Place on oiled grill pan over medium-high heat. Working in batches, cook octopus and squid for 3-5 minutes, just until cooked through. Combine octopus and calamari in medium heatproof bowl with remaining oil, vinegar and 2 tablespoons of the parsley. Cover to keep warm.

5 Cook shrimp and sardines on same grill pan.

6 Meanwhile, place a large skillet over medium-high heat. Add mussels and water; cook, covered for about 5 minutes or until mussels open (discard any that do not). Place mussels in medium heatproof bowl; drizzle with juice, sprinkle with tomato and remaining parsley. Arrange seafood on platter and serve with lemon wedges, if desired.

prep + cook time 1 hour (+ refrigeration) **serves** 8

bites & spreads

goat cheese and chive pastries
Preheat oven to 400°F (375°F convection). Combine 8 ounces soft goat cheese, ¼ cup finely chopped fresh chives, ¼ cup finely chopped toasted slivered almonds and ¼ cup finely chopped prunes in small bowl. Spray one of 16 sheets phyllo dough with cooking-oil spray. Top with another sheet. Repeat to make four stacks. Cut each stack into four to make 16 rectangles. Place level tablespoons of cheese mixture along short sides of each rectangle. Roll dough once over filling; fold in both sides then roll up to form cigars. Place pastries on baking sheet lined with parchment paper; bake 15 minutes.
prep + cook time 1 hour **makes** 16

blue cheese toasts with pear and watercress Preheat broiler. Cut 1 small loaf french bread into ½-inch slices. Brush bread both sides with combined 2 tablespoons melted butter and 1 clove crushed garlic; place bread, in single layer, on baking sheet. Broil bread, turning once, until both sides are browned. Thinly slice 1 medium pear. Spread toasts with 6 ounces soft blue cheese; top with pear slices and 1 cup trimmed watercress.
prep + cook time 30 minutes
makes 20

fig and quince paste Peel, core and quarter 2 pounds of quinces; combine in large saucepan with 1 cup chopped dried figs, 1 cinnamon stick and enough water to cover, bring to the boil. Simmer, covered, about 1 hour or until most liquid is absorbed. Discard cinnamon; process mixture until pulpy. Measure mixture into same pan. Add 1 cup sugar to every 1 cup pulp; stir in ¼ cup lemon juice, stir until sugar dissolves. Cook, over very low heat, 2 hours or until mixture leaves side of pan. Pour into oiled and lined deep 8-inch-round cake pan. Stand at room temperature overnight until set. Serve as part of a cheese platter.
prep + cook time 3½ hours (+ standing) **makes** 4 cups

blue cheese and caramelized onion dip Melt 1 tablespoon butter in medium saucepan; cook 1 coarsely chopped large onion, stirring, until onion softens. Add 2 tablespoons brown sugar and 2 tablespoons white wine vinegar; cook, stirring, over low heat, about 10 minutes or until onion is caramelized. Stir in 4 ounces crumbled blue cheese and ¾ cup crème fraîche until smooth. Cool. Cover; refrigerate until cold. Stir in ¼ cup finely chopped fresh flat-leaf parsley.
prep + cook time 30 minutes
makes 1½ cups

baked brie Preheat oven to 400°F (375°F convection). Coat 1 cup ovenproof dish (4 inches diameter, 2 inches deep.) Place whole 6 ounces brie in dish. Make six small slits into cheese. Cut 1 sprig fresh thyme into six pieces; push thyme into slits. Pour 2 tablespoons dry red wine over cheese; cover dish, place on oven tray. Bake 20 minutes. Stand, covered, 5 minutes. Sprinkle with 1 teaspoon fresh lemon zest and 1 finely chopped fresh thyme sprig to serve.
prep + cook time 40 minutes
serves 8

fried cauliflower

1 small cauliflower, cut into florets
3 eggs
½ cup milk
½ cup self-rising flour
¼ cup grated Parmesan cheese
2 tablespoons finely chopped fresh flat-leaf parsley
vegetable oil, for deep-frying
lemon wedges (optional)

1 Boil, steam or microwave cauliflower until tender; drain. Cool.
2 Whisk eggs, milk, flour, cheese and parsley in medium shallow bowl until smooth.
3 Heat oil in wok. Dip cauliflower into batter; drain off excess. Deep-fry cauliflower, in batches, until lightly browned. Drain on paper towels.
4 Serve cauliflower with lemon wedges, if desired.

prep + cook time 40 minutes **serves** 16

marinated mushrooms

4 cups white vinegar
1 cup dry white wine
1 tablespoon sea salt
1½ pounds button mushrooms, halved
2 cloves garlic, thinly sliced
½ teaspoon red pepper flakes
1 tablespoon coarsely chopped fresh rosemary
1 tablespoon finely chopped fresh flat-leaf parsley
3 strips (2 inches each) lemon rind
1 bay leaf
2 cups olive oil

1 Sterilize a 4-cup jar and lid.
2 Combine vinegar, wine and half the salt in medium
saucepan; heat without boiling. Add mushrooms;
simmer, uncovered, about 5 minutes or until tender.
Drain mushrooms; discard liquid.
3 Combine hot mushrooms, garlic, pepper flakes,
herbs, zest, bay leaf and remaining salt in large heatproof
bowl. Spoon mushroom mixture into hot sterilized jar.
4 Heat oil in small saucepan; carefully pour over
mushrooms in jar to completely cover mushrooms,
leaving a ½-inch space between mushrooms and top of
jar. Seal while hot.

prep + cook time 40 minutes **makes** 4 cups
Store marinated mushrooms in refrigerator for up to three
months. Serve mushrooms with crusty bread or as part
of an antipasto platter with cheeses and deli meats.

veal braciole

arancini

veal braciole

⅔ cup stale breadcrumbs
1 tablespoon rinsed drained baby capers,
    finely chopped
2 cloves garlic, crushed
5 veal scallops (1 pound)
1 lemon, quartered, thickly sliced
20 fresh bay leaves
1 tablespoon olive oil

1   Combine breadcrumbs, capers and garlic in small bowl.
2   Using meat mallet, gently pound veal, one piece at
a time, between sheets of parchment paper until ½-inch
thick; cut each piece in half crossways.
3   Press 1 level tablespoon of crumb mixture over one
side of each piece of veal. Roll veal up tightly; cut each
roll in half.
4   Thread lemon slices, veal rolls and bay leaves onto
20 small bamboo skewers or strong toothpicks. Place on
oiled grill plate over medium-high heat. Brush skewers all
over with oil; cook until veal is cooked through.

prep + cook time 40 minutes **makes** 20
You need 20 small bamboo skewers or strong toothpicks
for this recipe. Soak skewers in cold water at least an hour
before using to prevent them scorching during cooking.

arancini

2 cups chicken stock
½ cup dry white wine
2 tablespoons butter
1 small onion, finely chopped
1 clove garlic, crushed
1 cup arborio rice
⅓ cup grated Parmesan cheese
⅓ cup grated mozzarella cheese
24 pitted green olives
⅓ cup packaged breadcrumbs
vegetable oil, for deep-frying

1   Combine stock and wine in medium saucepan; bring
to the boil. Reduce heat; simmer, covered.
2   Meanwhile, melt butter in medium saucepan; cook
onion and garlic, stirring, until onion softens. Add rice;
stir over medium heat until rice is coated in butter
mixture. Stir in ½ cup of the simmering stock mixture;
cook, stirring, over low heat until liquid is absorbed.
Continue adding mixture, in ½ cup batches, stirring,
until liquid is absorbed after each addition. Total cooking
time should be about 35 minutes or until rice is tender.
Stir in cheeses, cover; cool 30 minutes.
3   Roll rounded tablespoons of risotto mixture into balls;
press an olive into center of each ball, roll to enclose.
Coat risotto balls in breadcrumbs.
4   Heat oil in wok; deep-fry risotto balls, in batches,
until lightly browned. Drain on paper towels.

prep + cook time 1 hour 30 minutes (+ cooling)
makes 24

risotto-filled zucchini flowers

2 cups chicken stock
½ cup (125ml) dry white wine
pinch saffron
2 tablespoons butter
1 small onion, finely chopped
1 clove garlic, crushed
1 cup arborio rice
⅓ cup grated Parmesan cheese
1 teaspoon fresh lemon zest
2 tablespoons finely chopped
   fresh flat-leaf parsley
28 zucchini flowers with stem attached
cooking-oil spray

1 Combine stock, wine and saffron in medium saucepan; bring to the boil. Reduce heat; simmer, covered.
2 Meanwhile, melt butter in medium saucepan; cook onion and garlic, stirring, until onion softens. Add rice; stir over medium heat until rice is coated in butter mixture. Stir in ½ cup of the simmering stock mixture; cook, stirring, over low heat until liquid is absorbed. Continue adding stock mixture, in ½ cup batches, stirring, until liquid is absorbed after each addition. Total cooking time should be about 35 minutes or until rice is tender. Stir in cheese, zest and parsley, cover; cool 30 minutes.
3 Preheat oven to 400°F (375°F convection). Coat two baking sheets with cooking spray.
4 Discard stamens from zucchini flowers; fill flowers with 1 level tablespoon of risotto mixture, twist petal tops to enclose filling.
5 Place zucchini flowers on trays; spray all over with cooking spray. Roast, uncovered, about 15 minutes or until zucchini stems are tender.

prep + cook time 1 hour 30 minutes (+ cooking)
makes 28
If you don't want to make 28 zucchini flowers – just eat the delicious risotto as it is.

tomato tarts

4 vine-ripened tomatoes,
  peeled, quartered, pitted
1 tablespoon brown sugar
1 tablespoon balsamic vinegar
½ sheet frozen puff pastry, thawed
16 sprigs fresh chervil

1 Preheat oven 425°F (400°F convection).
2 Combine tomato, sugar and vinegar in small baking dish; roast, uncovered, about 20 minutes or until tomato is soft.
3 Meanwhile, cut pastry sheet in half lengthways, cut each half into 4 squares; cut each square into triangles (you will have 16). Lightly oil a baking sheet. Arrange pastry triangles on sheet and top with another baking sheet (the second sheet stops the pastry from puffing up). Bake pastry, alongside tomato, about 10 minutes or until crisp.
4 Place a tomato piece on each pastry triangle. Serve topped with chervil.

prep + cook time 40 minutes **makes** 16

sweet and sour beets

2 large beets, peeled, coarsely grated
3 scallions, thinly sliced
1 tablespoon finely chopped fresh dill
2 tablespoons red wine vinegar
1 tablespoon olive oil
1 teaspoon wholegrain mustard
2 teaspoons sugar
1 red endive, leaves separated (see note)

1 Combine beets, onion, dill, vinegar, oil, mustard and sugar in medium bowl.
2 Serve beets mixture with endive.

prep time 15 minutes **makes** 24
You need 24 endive leaves for this recipe.

meatballs napolitana

1 pound ground beef
1 egg
½ cup packaged breadcrumbs
¼ cup grated Parmesan cheese
¼ cup finely chopped fresh flat-leaf parsley
2 tablespoons olive oil
1 small onion, finely chopped
1 clove garlic, crushed
1 jar (24 ounces) tomato pasta sauce
½ cup frozen peas
¼ cup coarsely chopped fresh basil
crusty bread (optional)

1 Combine beef, egg, breadcrumbs, cheese and parsley in medium bowl. Using wet hands, roll level tablespoons of beef mixture into balls.
2 Heat half the oil in large skillet; cook meatballs, in batches, until browned and cooked through.
3 Heat remaining oil in same pan; cook onion and garlic, stirring, until onion softens. Add sauce; bring to the boil. Add meatballs, reduce heat; simmer, uncovered, about 10 minutes or until sauce thickens slightly. Add peas and basil; simmer, uncovered, until peas are tender.
4 Serve meatballs and sauce with crusty bread, if desired.

prep + cook time 1 hour **makes** 26

fish and caper croquettes

¾ cup water

¾ cup dry white wine

2 bay leaves

3/4 pound skinless firm white fish fillets

2 tablespoons butter

¼ cup all-purpose flour

1 cup milk

2 teaspoons fresh lemon zest

2 tablespoons rinsed drained baby capers,
   finely chopped

1 clove garlic, crushed

1 tablespoon finely chopped fresh chives

¼ cup all-purpose flour, extra

1 egg, beaten lightly

1 cup stale breadcrumbs

vegetable oil, for shallow-frying

1 medium lemon, thickly sliced

1 Combine the water, wine and bay leaves in small saucepan; bring to the boil. Add fish, reduce heat; simmer, covered, about 5 minutes or until fish is cooked through. Drain fish; discard cooking liquid, flake fish coarsely.

2 Meanwhile, melt butter in medium saucepan. Add flour; cook, stirring, about 2 minutes or until mixture thickens and bubbles. Gradually stir in milk; cook, stirring, until mixture boils and thickens. Remove from heat; stir in zest, capers, garlic, chives and fish. Cover; refrigerate 2 hours.

3 Roll rounded tablespoons of fish mixture into ovals; coat in extra flour, shake off excess. Dip croquettes in egg then breadcrumbs.

4 Heat oil in large skillet; cook croquettes until browned all over. Drain on paper towels. Serve with lemon slices.

prep + cook time 40 minutes (+ refrigeration)
makes 16

mezze

chicken, spinach and cheese gözleme

2 cups all-purpose flour
½ teaspoon salt
¾ cup warm water
2 tablespoons olive oil
1 onion, finely chopped
2 cloves garlic, crushed
2 teaspoons ground cumin
1 teaspoon ground cinnamon
5 ounces spinach, trimmed
1 cup finely shredded cooked chicken
4 ounces feta cheese, crumbled
2 tablespoons lemon juice
lemon wedges (optional)

1 Combine flour and salt in medium bowl. Gradually stir in the water; mix to a soft dough. Knead dough on floured surface about 5 minutes or until smooth and elastic. Return to bowl; cover, while preparing filling.

2 Heat half the oil in medium skillet; cook onion and garlic, stirring, until onion softens. Add spices; cook, stirring, until fragrant. Transfer mixture to medium heatproof bowl; cool.

3 Meanwhile, boil, steam or microwave spinach until wilted; rinse under cold water, drain. Squeeze out excess water; shred spinach finely. Stir spinach, chicken, cheese and juice into onion mixture.

4 Divide dough in half; roll each piece on floured surface into 10 x 14 inch rectangle. Divide spinach filling across center of each rectangle. Fold top and bottom edges of dough over filling; tuck in ends to enclose.

5 Place on oiled grill pan over low heat. Cook gözleme, both sides, brushing with remaining oil until lightly browned and heated through. Stand 5 minutes before cutting each gözleme into 8 slices; serve with lemon wedges, if desired.

prep + cook time 1 hour 30 minutes **makes** 16

fried fish sandwiches

grilled baby octopus

fried fish sandwiches

2 cloves garlic, unpeeled
½ cup Greek-style yogurt
¼ cup finely chopped fresh mint
8 small white fish fillets (about ¾ pound), skin on
2 tablespoons all-purpose flour
2 teaspoons smoked paprika
1 teaspoon ground cumin
1 tablespoon olive oil
1 loaf turkish bread, split, toasted
1 head baby romaine, leaves separated
2 tomatoes, thinly sliced
½ small red onion, thinly sliced

1 Preheat oven to 400°F (375°F convection).
2 Place garlic on oven tray; roast, uncovered, about 10 minutes or until soft. Cool; peel garlic.
3 Blend or process garlic and yogurt until smooth; stir in mint.
4 Coat fish in combined flour and spices; shake off excess. Heat oil in large skillet; cook fish, both sides, until browned and crisp.
5 Spread yogurt over one half of bread; top with lettuce, tomato, onion, fish and remaining bread. Cut into 12 slices.

prep + cook time 30 minutes makes 12

grilled baby octopus

2 pounds frozen baby octopus, thawed
⅓ cup lemon juice
⅓ cup olive oil
2 cloves garlic, crushed
1 tablespoon dried oregano
1 medium lemon, cut into wedges

1 Rinse octopus in cold water and ensure it is clean by, removing eyes and beaks if necessary. Combine octopus with juice, oil, garlic and oregano in medium bowl. Cover, refrigerate 3 hours or overnight.
2 Drain octopus; discard marinade. Place on oiled grill pan over medium-high heat. Cook octopus until tender. Serve with lemon wedges.

prep + cook time 25 minutes (+ refrigeration) serves 6
Octopus is best cooked just before serving.

radish and herb salad

4 pita breads (6-inches each), cut into wedges
1 green bell pepper, finely chopped
1 cucumber, seeded, finely chopped
1 tomato, finely chopped
4 red radishes, coarsely grated
½ cup finely chopped fresh flat-leaf parsley
⅓ cup finely chopped fresh mint
¼ cup coarsely chopped fresh cilantro
2 tablespoons olive oil
2 tablespoons lemon juice
2 cloves garlic, minced

1 Preheat broiler.
2 Place bread on baking sheet; broil about 5 minutes or until browned both sides and crisp.
3 Combine remaining ingredients in medium bowl. Serve salad with pita crisps.

prep + cook time 25 minutes **serves** 8

spicy tunisian tuna salad

2 teaspoons caraway seeds

½ teaspoon ground cinnamon

1 can tuna (12 ounces) in oil

1 can (15 ounces) chickpeas, rinsed, drained

1 small green bell pepper, cut into ½-inch pieces

⅓ cup pitted black olives, coarsely chopped

1 pint red grape tomatoes, quartered

2 scallions, thinly sliced

2 teaspoons fresh orange zest

2 tablespoons orange juice

1 tablespoon harissa

Turkish bread

1 Toast spices in small skillet over medium-high heat until fragrant; cool.

2 Drain tuna; reserve 2 tablespoons of the oil. Flake tuna coarsely.

3 Combine tuna, reserved oil, spices and remaining ingredients in large bowl. Serve with toasted Turkish bread.

prep + cook time 25 minutes serves 8

pickled octopus

2 pounds frozen chopped octopus, thawed
¾ cup extra virgin olive oil
½ cup white wine vinegar
1 clove garlic, crushed
2 tablespoons coarsely chopped
   fresh flat-leaf parsley
lemon wedges (optional)

1 Place octopus in large saucepan with 1 cup water. Cover pan, cook over low heat about 1 hour or until octopus is tender. Cool octopus in pan until it is cool enough to handle.
2 Transfer octopus to medium bowl with remaining ingredients. Cover, refrigerate overnight. Serve sprinkled with parsley; accompany with lemon wedges, if desired.

prep + cook time 1 hour 10 minutes (+ cooling and refrigeration) **serves** 8
You could also use baby octopus in this recipe if you prefer. Recipe can be made up to four days ahead; store, covered, in the refrigerator.

blood orange and chile glazed quail

6 quails (about 2 pounds)
1 teaspoon cumin seeds
½ cup blood orange juice
1 fresh long red chile, finely chopped
1 clove garlic, crushed
2 tablespoons brown sugar
1 tablespoon finely chopped fresh cilantro

1 Using kitchen scissors, cut along both sides of quails' backbones; discard backbones. Halve each quail along breastbone; cut each in half again to give a total of 24 pieces.
2 Place on oiled grill pan over medium-high heat. Cook quail, covered, about 20 minutes or until cooked through.
3 Meanwhile, toast seeds in a small dry skillet over medium-high heat until fragrant. Add juice, chile, garlic and sugar; stir over heat, without boiling, until sugar dissolves. Bring to the boil; boil, uncovered, about 5 minutes or until mixture is thick and syrupy.
4 Combine hot quail, syrup and cilantro in large bowl.

prep + cook time 35 minutes **serves** 8
Quails are available from gourmet grocery stores and some farmer's markets.

lemon pepper squid

1 pound frozen squid hoods, thawed
½ cup all-purpose flour
2 tablespoons lemon pepper seasoning
1 tablespoon dried oregano
1 teaspoon kosher salt
peanut oil, for deep-frying
1 tablespoon coarsely chopped fresh parsley

1 Cut squid down center to open flat; score inside in diagonal pattern then cut into thick strips.
2 Combine flour, lemon pepper, oregano and salt in large bowl; add squid, toss to coat in mixture, shake away excess.
3 Heat oil in deep saucepan; deep-fry squid, in batches, until tender. Drain on paper towels. Serve sprinkled with parsley.

prep + cook time 30 minutes **serves** 4
Lemon pepper seasoning is a blend of crushed black pepper, lemon, herbs and spices. It's available from the dried herb and spice section at most supermarkets. If you use one containing salt, reduce the salt quantity in this recipe.

blood orange and chile glazed quail

lemon pepper squid

turkish tomato salad

1 teaspoon cumin seeds
2 tomatoes, finely chopped
1 red bell pepper, finely chopped
1 small red onion, finely chopped
1 fresh long red chile, finely chopped
¼ cup finely chopped fresh flat-leaf parsley
1 tablespoon pomegranate molasses
2 tablespoons olive oil
Turkish bread (optional)

1 Toast seeds in a small dry skillet over medium-high heat until fragrant; cool.
2 Combine seeds with remaining ingredients in medium bowl. Serve with toasted Turkish bread if desired.

prep + cook time 20 minutes **serves** 8

grilled haloumi

1 pound haloumi cheese
2 tablespoons lemon juice
1 tablespoon coarsely chopped
   fresh flat-leaf parsley

1 Cut cheese into ½-inch slices. Place on oiled grill pan over medium-high heat (use the flat side if your pan has one). Cook cheese until browned both sides.
2 Transfer cheese to serving plate; drizzle with juice. Serve immediately, sprinkled with parsley.

prep + cook time 10 minutes **serves** 6
Haloumi is best cooked just before serving as it becomes tough and rubbery on cooling.

cheese pastries

1½ cups all-purpose flour
1½ cups self-rising flour
½ teaspoon salt
¾ cup warm water
¼ cup olive oil
1 egg, lightly beaten
2 teaspoons sesame seeds
filling
1 egg, beaten lightly
4 ounces feta cheese, crumbled
½ cup ricotta cheese
½ cup finely grated romano cheese

1 Preheat oven to 400°F (375°F convection). Line two baking sheets with parchment paper.
2 Process flours and salt until combined. While motor is running, add enough of the combined water and oil so the mixture forms a ball (do not overmix). Remove dough from bowl, wrap in plastic; cover, refrigerate 30 minutes.
3 Meanwhile, make filling.
4 Divide dough in half. Roll each half on floured surface to 12 x 16 inch rectangle; cut 13 3-inch rounds from each rectangle of dough. Drop rounded teaspoons of filling onto rounds; brush edges with a little water. Fold rounds in half, press edges together with a fork to seal. Place pastries on trays; brush with egg, sprinkle with seeds. Bake about 15 minutes or until lightly browned.
filling Combine ingredients in medium bowl.

prep + cook time 1 hour 15 minutes (+ refrigeration)
makes 26
Parmesan cheese can be used instead of romano cheese. Pastries can be served warm or cold. Uncooked pastries are suitable to freeze. It is best to cut pastry into the 26 rounds from the first rolling of pastry, as the pastry is not suitable to reroll.

skewers

Soak skewers in water for at least an hour prior to using to prevent them from scorching during cooking.

lemon, garlic and oregano lamb skewers Cut 1½ pounds boneless lamb loin into 1-inch pieces. Combine lamb in medium bowl with 1 tablespoon olive oil, 2 teaspoons fresh lemon zest, 1 clove crushed garlic and 2 tablespoons finely chopped fresh oregano. Cover; refrigerate 1 hour. Stir in 1 tablespoon lemon juice. Thread lamb onto 16 small bamboo skewers or strong toothpicks. Place on oiled grill pan over medium-high heat; cook until lamb is cooked through.
prep + cook time 30 minutes (+ refrigeration) **makes** 16

sumac and sesame chicken skewers Cut 1 pound boneless, skinless chicken breast into 1-inch cubes; thread onto 16 small bamboo skewers or strong toothpicks. Combine 1 tablespoon sumac, 1 teaspoon sesame seeds and 1 teaspoon black sesame seeds in small bowl; sprinkle sumac mixture all over skewers. Place on oiled grill pan over medium-high heat; cook skewers until chicken is cooked through. Serve with lemon wedges.
prep + cook time 30 minutes **makes** 16
Sumac is a purple-red, astringent spice ground from wild Mediterranean berries; it adds a tart, lemony flavor.

vegetable and haloumi skewers
Cut 6 ounces haloumi cheese into sixteen 1-inch cubes; cut 1 small red bell pepper into 1-inch pieces. Cut 1 large zucchini in half lengthways; cut each half into eight 1-inch pieces. Thread haloumi, bell pepper and zucchini onto 16 small bamboo skewers or strong toothpicks. Place on oiled grill pan over medium-high heat; cook skewers until vegetables are tender. Meanwhile, combine ½ cup mayonnaise, 1 tablespoon lime juice and 2 teaspoons harissa in small bowl. Serve skewers with mayonnaise.
prep + cook time 35 minutes
makes 16

lamb kebabs with yogurt and pita bread Combine 1 pound ground lamb, 1 egg, 1 finely chopped small onion, 2 tablespoons finely chopped fresh flat-leaf parsley, 1 crushed clove garlic, 2 teaspoons each ground cinnamon and sweet paprika and ½ teaspoon cayenne pepper in bowl. Form lamb mixture into 16 sausage shapes, thread onto 16 small bamboo skewers or strong toothpicks; flatten slightly. Place on oiled grill pan over medium-high heat; cook kebabs until browned and cooked through. Serve kebabs with ½ cup yogurt, lemon wedges and pita bread.
prep + cook time 30 minutes
serves 4 (makes 16 skewers)

chermoulla shrimp skewers Shell and devein 16 uncooked large shrimp king shrimp, leaving tails intact. Combine shrimp with 1 tablespoon olive oil, 2 tablespoons each finely chopped fresh flat-leaf parsley, mint and cilantro, 2 cloves crushed garlic, 2 teaspoons fresh lemon zest, 1 tablespoon lemon juice, 1 teaspoon ground allspice and 1 teaspoon caraway seeds in medium bowl. Preheat broiler. Thread shrimp, tail-end first, onto 16 small bamboo skewers or strong toothpicks and arrange on broiler tray; broil shrimp 5 minutes or until changed in color.
prep + cook time 30 minutes
makes 16

greek eggplant dip

rosewater and sesame chicken drumettes

greek eggplant dip

2 large eggplants (1 pound each), unpeeled
1 tablespoon kosher salt
¼ cup olive oil
½ cup Greek-style yogurt
1 white onion, coarsely grated
⅓ cup coarsely chopped fresh flat-leaf parsley
2 tablespoons lemon juice
2 cloves garlic, crushed

1 Cut eggplant into ½-inch slices. Place in colander, sprinkle with salt; stand 30 minutes. Rinse eggplant under cold water; drain on paper towels.
2 Preheat broiler.
3 Working in batches, brush both sides of eggplant with oil and arrange on broiler tray; broil, turning halfway through, until browned both sides and tender. When cool enough to handle remove skin from eggplant.
4 Process eggplant with remaining ingredients until combined. Refrigerate 3 hours or overnight.

prep + cook time 45 minutes (+ standing and refrigeration) makes 1½ cups
Serve dip with fresh crusty bread. Dip can be made three days ahead; store, covered, in the refrigerator.

rosewater and sesame chicken drumettes

20 chicken drumettes (about 3 pounds)
2 tablespoons brown sugar
⅓ cup rosewater
1 tablespoon olive oil
½ teaspoon ground allspice
2 teaspoons sesame seeds

1 Using small sharp knife pierce chicken all over. Combine chicken, sugar, rosewater, oil and spice in large bowl. Cover; refrigerate 3 hours or overnight.
2 Preheat oven to 425°F (400°F convection).
3 Place chicken on oiled wire rack over large baking dish; pour over any remaining marinade, sprinkle with seeds. Roast chicken, uncovered, basting with pan juices occasionally, 30 minutes or until cooked through.

prep + cook time 35 minutes (+ refrigeration)
makes 20

spinach and feta triangles

2 teaspoons olive oil

3 scallions, finely chopped

½ pound baby spinach leaves

8 ounces feta cheese, crumbled

2 tablespoons finely chopped
   fresh flat-leaf parsley

1 tablespoon finely chopped fresh dill

1 egg

1 pound frozen phyllo dough (20 sheets), thawed

5 tablespoons butter, melted

1 Heat oil in large skillet, add onion; cook, stirring, until onion is softened. Add spinach; cook, stirring, until spinach is wilted. Remove from heat. When cool enough to handle, squeeze excess moisture from spinach; chop coarsely.

2 Combine spinach mixture in medium bowl with cheese, herbs and egg.

3 Preheat oven to 400°F (375°F convection). Line baking sheets with parchment paper.

4 Brush 1 sheet of pastry with melted butter; top with a second sheet and brush with melted butter. Cut layered sheets into
4 strips lengthways. Place rounded teaspoons of spinach mixture at one end of each strip. Fold one corner of pastry diagonally over filling to form a triangle. Continue folding to end of strip, retaining triangular shape. Brush triangles with a little butter. Repeat to make a total of 40 triangles.

5 Place triangles on trays. Bake about 15 minutes or until lightly browned.

prep + cook time 1 hour 30 minutes **makes** 48
To prevent dough from drying out, cover with plastic wrap or a damp tea towel until ready to use. Uncooked triangles are suitable to freeze.

beet and yogurt dip

1 pound beets
½ cup Greek-style yogurt
1 clove garlic, crushed
2 tablespoons lemon juice
2 tablespoons coarsely chopped fresh mint
pita bread

1 Preheat oven to 400°F (375°F convection). Line baking sheet with parchment paper.
2 Wash beets well, cut off leaves. Place unpeeled beets on baking sheet. Roast about 1 hour or until tender. When beets are cool enough to handle, peel and chop coarsely; cool.
3 Process beets. Add remaining ingredients; process until smooth. Serve dip with torn pieces of heated pita bread.

prep + cook time 1 hour 30 minutes **makes** 1⅓ cups
Dip can be made up to two days ahead;
store, covered, in the refrigerator.

spicy tomatoes

¼ cup coarsely chopped fresh flat-leaf parsley
2 cloves garlic, crushed
½ teaspoon red pepper flakes
2 tablespoons olive oil
4 large roma tomatoes, thickly sliced

1 Combine parsley, garlic and pepper flakes in small bowl.
2 Heat oil in large skillet, carefully add tomato in a single layer; cook, over high heat, 2 minutes. Turn tomato, sprinkle with parsley mixture; cook, shaking pan occasionally, about 1 minute or until tomato is caramelized but still holding its shape.
3 Transfer to serving plate; drizzle with pan juices.

prep + cook time 15 minutes **serves** 6
Take care when adding tomato to pan as it may splatter. Tomato is best cooked just before serving.

broiled feta

8 ounces feta cheese
2 teaspoons olive oil
½ teaspoon sweet paprika
1 loaf ciabatta bread (1 pound), cut into 1-inch
   slices
¼ cup olive oil, extra
2 teaspoons coarsely chopped fresh oregano

1 Preheat broiler.
2 Pat cheese dry with paper towels. Place cheese on
baking sheet; brush top and sides with combined oil
and paprika. Broil cheese until lightly browned.

3 Lightly brush both sides of bread with extra oil and
arrange on another baking sheet. Toast bread under
broiler, turning once, until browned both sides.
4 Sprinkle warm cheese with oregano; serve with
toasted bread.

prep + cook time 20 minutes **serves** 8
*Any thick crusty-style bread can be used. Do not line
baking sheetswith parchment paper as it may burn during
broiling.*

labne

sardines with caper and parsley topping

labne

You need a 10-inch piece cheesecloth for this recipe.

2 cups Greek-style yogurt
1½ teaspoons fine table salt
1 tablespoon extra virgin olive oil
½ teaspoon red pepper flakes
1 tablespoon coarsely chopped cilantro
1 tablespoon coarsely chopped fresh mint

1 Combine yogurt and salt in medium bowl. Place a 5-inch diameter strainer over bowl. Rinse cheesecloth in hot water; wring out then line strainer. Place yogurt into strainer; cover with plastic wrap. Refrigerate at least 24 hours to allow to drain.
2 Turn labne onto serving plate, remove cheesecloth; drizzle labne with oil, sprinkle with pepper flakes, cilantro and mint.

prep time 10 minutes (+ refrigeration) **serves** 8
Labne can be drained longer than 24 hours, in fact, 48 hours is better; the longer it is drained the firmer it will become.

sardines with caper and parsley topping

8 sardines (about ¾ pound), cleaned
⅓ cup self-rising flour
½ teaspoon sweet paprika
¼ cup olive oil
lemon wedges (optional)
caper and parsley topping
2 tablespoons rinsed, drained baby capers, finely chopped
1 clove garlic, crushed
¼ cup finely chopped fresh flat-leaf parsley
2 teaspoons fresh lemon zest
2 teaspoons lemon juice

1 Make caper and parsley topping.
2 To butterfly sardines, cut through the underside of the fish to the tail. Break backbone at tail; peel away backbone. Trim sardines.
3 Coat fish in combined flour and paprika; shake away excess. Heat oil in large skillet; cook in batches, until cooked through, drain on paper towels.
4 Sprinkle fish with caper and parsley topping. Serve with lemon wedges, if desired.
caper and parsley topping Combine ingredients in small bowl.

prep + cook time 45 minutes **serves** 8
The caper and parsley topping is best made on the day of serving; store, covered, in the refrigerator until ready to use.

focaccia

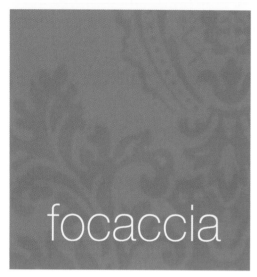

basic focaccia dough Combine 2¼ teaspoons active dry yeast, 1 teaspoon sugar, ⅔ cup warm water and 2 tablespoons warm milk in a glass measuring cup. Stand in warm place until frothy. Place ½ cup all-purpose flour in bowl; whisk in yeast mixture. Cover; stand in warm place 1 hour. Stir 1½ cups all-purpose flour and 1 teaspoon salt into yeast mixture with 1 tablespoon olive oil. Knead dough on floured surface until smooth. Place in oiled bowl, cover; stand in warm place 1 hour. Make focaccia. Preheat oven to 475°F (450°F convection). Roll dough into 14-inch oval; place dough on parchment paper. Make indents with finger and brush over 1 tablespoon olive oil; sprinkle with 2 teaspoons black sesame seeds. Heat baking sheet; lift dough onto tray on paper; bake focaccia about 15 minutes.
prep + cook time 30 minutes (+ standing) **serves** 8

egg and cheese focaccia Preheat oven to 475°F (450°F convection). Divide 1 batch basic focaccia dough into three pieces; roll each piece to 5 x 12 inches. Brush edges of dough with water; fold 1-inch border around edges of dough, press down firmly. Fold in corners to make oval shape. Heat baking sheet in oven for 3 minutes. Quickly place focaccia on hot sheets; bake 5 minutes. Remove from oven; press center of focaccia with spatula down to flatten. Whisk 3 eggs with 3 ounces coarsely grated haloumi cheese and 1 finely chopped scallion in small bowl. Pour into the cavities of the focaccia. Bake 10 minutes or until set. Cut each focaccia into eight slices; serve with lemon wedges.
prep + cook time 25 minutes **serves** 8

lamb and tomato focaccia Preheat oven to 475°F (450°F convection). Heat
1 tablespoon olive oil in pan; cook 1 chopped onion and 1 clove crushed garlic. Add ½ pound ground lamb, 1 teaspoon each ground cinnamon, cumin and smoked paprika and ½ teaspoon cayenne pepper; cook until lamb is browned. Stir in 1 tablespoon chopped fresh cilantro; cool. Divide 1 batch basic dough into three; roll each piece to 5 x 12 iches. Spread filling across center of each piece, leaving 1-inch border. Brush edges with water; fold and press around dough. Fold corners to make oval shape. Heat baking sheets 3 minutes, place focaccia on sheets; bake 10 minutes. Sprinkle with 1 chopped tomato; bake 5 minutes.
prep + cook time 35 minutes
serves 8

spinach and feta focaccia Preheat oven to 475°F (450°F convection). Boil, steam or microwave ½ pound spinach until wilted. Rinse, drain then squeeze out excess water; shred spinach finely. Combine spinach, 4 ounces crumbled feta cheese and 4 ounces coarsely grated haloumi cheese in medium bowl. Divide 1 batch basic dough into three; roll each to 5 x 12 inches. Spread filling across center of each piece, leaving 1-inch border. Brush edges with water;
fold and press around dough. Fold corners to make oval shape. Heat baking sheets 3 minutes, place focaccia on sheets; bake 15 minutes. Cut each focaccia into eight slices.
prep + cook time 25 minutes
serves 8

pumpkin and feta focaccia Preheat oven to 475°F (450°F convection). Boil, steam or microwave ½ pound chopped butternut squash until tender; drain, cool. Combine squash, 4 ounces chopped feta cheese and ½ cup grated mozzarella cheese in medium bowl. Divide 1 batch basic dough into three; roll each to 5 x 12 inch. Spread filling across center of each piece, leaving 1-inch border. Brush edges with water; fold and press around dough. Fold corners to make oval shape. Heat baking sheets 3 minutes, place focaccia on sheets; bake 15 minutes. Top with 1 tablespoon finely chopped fresh flat-leaf parsley. Cut each focaccia into eight slices.
prep + cook time 30 minutes
serves 8

zucchini fritters with skordalia

4 zucchini (about 1 pound)
2 teaspoons kosher salt
peanut oil, for deep-frying
skordalia
4 slices stale white sandwich bread,
  crusts removed
4 cloves garlic, crushed
½ cup olive oil
1 tablespoon lemon juice
1 tablespoon water, approximately
batter
1 cup self-rising flour
¾ cup warm water
1 tablespoon olive oil
1 egg yolk

1 Make skordalia.
2 Cut zucchini into ½-inch diagonal slices. Place zucchini in colander, sprinkle with salt; stand 30 minutes. Rinse zucchini under cold water; drain on paper towels.
3 Make batter.
4 Heat oil in large deep skillet. Dip zucchini into batter, carefully lower into hot oil; cook zucchini until browned and crisp; drain on paper towels.
5 Serve zucchini fritters with skordalia.

skordalia Briefly dip bread into a bowl of cold water, then gently squeeze out the water. Blend or process bread and garlic until combined. With motor running, gradually add oil, juice and enough of the water, in a thin steady stream, until mixture is smooth and thick. Transfer to serving bowl.

batter Sift flour into medium bowl; whisk in combined remaining ingredients until smooth. Stand batter 10 minutes. If batter thickens too much, whisk in a little extra water to give it a coating consistency.

prep + cook time 1 hour (+ standing) **serves** 6
Zucchini fritters are best made just before serving. Skordalia is best made on the day of serving; keep, covered, in the refrigerator.

mini baked herb ricotta

mini chicken souvlakia

mini baked herb ricotta

8 ounces ricotta cheese

1 egg

1 tablespoon finely chopped fresh flat-leaf parsley

1 teaspoon finely chopped fresh thyme

1 clove garlic, crushed

1 Preheat oven to 350°F (325°F convection). Coat 18 holes of two 12-hole (1½-tablespoons) mini muffin pans with cooking spray.

2 Blend or process ingredients until smooth. Divide mixture into pan holes. Bake about 20 minutes or until lightly browned.

prep + cook time 30 minutes **makes** 18

Serve mini baked ricottas warm or cold. Recipe can be made a day ahead; store, covered, in the refrigerator.

mini chicken souvlakia

2 pounds boneless, skinless chicken thigh

2 tablespoons olive oil

2 tablespoons lemon juice

⅓ cup finely chopped fresh mint

2 cloves garlic, crushed

1½ teaspoons smoked paprika

lemon wedges (optional)

1 Trim any fat from chicken; cut chicken into 1-inch thick strips. Combine chicken in medium bowl with remaining ingredients. Thread chicken onto 20 bamboo skewers; cover, refrigerate 3 hours or overnight.

2 Place on oiled grill pan over medium-high heat. Cook skewers until browned and cooked through. Serve with lemon wedges, if desired.

prep + cook time 35 minutes (+ refrigeration)

makes 20

Soak the skewers in cold water for at least an hour before using to prevent them from scorching during cooking. For optimum flavor, marinate the chicken overnight.

turkish lamb phyllo cigars

2 tablespoons olive oil
1 onion, finely chopped
2 cloves garlic, crushed
2 teaspoons ground allspice
2 teaspoons ground cilantro
1½ teaspoons ground cinnamon
1 teaspoon ground cumin
½ pound lean ground lamb
1 tablespoon lemon juice
6 sheets frozen phyllo dough, thawed
8 tablespoons (1 stick) butter, melted
mint yogurt
½ cup Greek-style yogurt
1 tablespoon finely chopped fresh mint

1 Heat oil in medium skillet, add onion and garlic; cook, stirring, until onion softens. Add spices; cook, stirring, until fragrant. Add lamb; cook, stirring until lamb is cooked through. Stir in juice; cool.
2 Preheat oven to 425°F (400°F convection). Coat baking sheet with cooking spray and line with parchment paper.
3 Brush 1 sheet of phyllo with butter; top with two more sheets, brushing each with butter. Cut layered sheets into 8 rectangles. Press 1 tablespoon of lamb mixture into a log shape along one long end of each rectangle. Roll pastry over filling; fold in sides then roll up to form a cigar shape. Repeat to make a total of 16 cigar shapes.
4 Place cigars, about 1-inch apart, on oven tray, brush with remaining butter. Bake about 15 minutes or until lightly browned.
5 Meanwhile, make mint yogurt.
6 Serve warm cigars with mint yogurt.
mint yogurt Combine ingredients in small bowl.

prep + cook time 1 hour 30 minutes **makes** 16
To prevent phyllo dough from drying out, cover with plastic
wrap then top with a damp tea-towel until ready to use.
Uncooked phyllo cigars are suitable to freeze.

fava bean dip

1 pound frozen fava beans
1 clove garlic, crushed
1 teaspoon ground cumin
½ teaspoon smoked paprika
2 tablespoons olive oil
1 tablespoon lemon juice
1 tablespoon finely chopped fresh mint
1 tablespoon olive oil, extra
¼ teaspoon smoked paprika, extra

1 Cook beans in medium saucepan of boiling water until tender; drain, reserving some of the cooking liquid. When cool enough to handle, peel away gray-colored outer shells from beans.
2 Blend or process beans with garlic, spices, oil, juice, mint and enough of the reserved cooking liquid until mixture is smooth.
3 Serve dip drizzled with extra oil and sprinkled with extra paprika.

prep + cook time 20 minutes **makes** 1¾ cups
Dip can be made a day ahead; store, covered, in the refrigerator.

char-grilled banana chiles

4 red banana chiles
1 tablespoon white wine vinegar
1 tablespoon olive oil
2 teaspoons finely chopped fresh flat-leaf parsley

1 Preheat broiler.
2 Cook whole chiles under broiler until blistered and blackened. Transfer to a large glass bowl. Cover for 5 minutes; peel away skin.
3 Arrange whole chiles on serving plate; drizzle with combined vinegar, oil and parsley.

prep + cook time 30 minutes **serves** 4
Recipe can be made a day ahead; store, covered, in the refrigerator.

dolmades

2 tablespoons olive oil
2 onions, finely chopped
¼ pound ground lean lamb
¾ cup white long-grain rice
2 tablespoons pine nuts
½ cup finely chopped fresh flat-leaf parsley
2 tablespoons finely chopped fresh dill
2 tablespoons finely chopped fresh mint
2 tablespoons lemon juice
2 cups water
1 jar (16 ounces) divided grape leaves
1 tablespoon lemon juice, extra
¾ cup yogurt

1 Heat oil in large saucepan, add onion; cook, stirring, until softened. Add lamb; cook, stirring, until lamb is browned. Stir in rice and pine nuts. Add herbs, juice and 1 cup water. Bring to the boil; reduce heat, simmer, covered, about 10 minutes or until water is absorbed and rice is partially cooked. Cool.

2 Rinse grape leaves in cold water. Drop into a large saucepan of boiling water, in batches, for a few seconds, transfer to colander; rinse under cold water, drain well.

3 Place a vine leaf, smooth side down on work surface, trim large stem. Place a heaped teaspoon of rice mixture in center. Fold stem end and sides over filling; roll up firmly. Line medium heavy-based saucepan with a few vine leaves, place rolls, close together, seam side down on leaves.

4 Pour the remaining cup of water over top of rolls; cover rolls with any remaining vine leaves. Place a plate on top of the leaves to keep rolls under the water during cooking. Cover pan tightly, bring to the boil; reduce heat, simmer, over very low heat, 1½ hours. Remove from heat; stand, covered about 2 hours or until all the liquid has been absorbed.

5 Serve with combined extra juice and yogurt.

prep + cook time 3 hours (+ standing) **serves** 10
Use any torn or damaged leaves to line the base of the pan and to cover the rolls. If you don't have enough vine leaves to cover the rolls in the pan, use a circle of baking paper, then top with the plate. Dolmades are best made a day ahead; store, covered, in the refrigerator.

mini falafel with tomato salsa

greek meatballs

mini falafel with tomato salsa

1 can (15 ounces) chickpeas, rinsed, drained
1 small white onion, finely chopped
½ cup finely chopped fresh flat-leaf parsley
2 tablespoons finely chopped fresh cilantro
2 teaspoons ground cumin
2 teaspoons ground cilantro
1 tablespoon fresh lemon zest
1 teaspoon salt
¼ cup all-purpose flour
peanut oil, for deep-frying
tomato salsa
1 roma tomato, finely chopped
1 tablespoon coarsely chopped fresh cilantro
1 tablespoon olive oil

1 To make falafel, blend or process chickpeas, onion, herbs, spices, zest and salt until coarsely chopped. Add flour; process until mixture forms a paste. Transfer mixture to medium bowl; cover, refrigerate 1 hour.
2 Make tomato salsa.
3 Shape falafel mixture between two teaspoons into oval shapes. Heat oil in medium deep skillet; cook falafel, in batches, until browned. Drain on paper towels.
4 Serve falafel with tomato salsa.
tomato salsa Combine ingredients in small bowl.

prep + cook time 1 hour 30 minutes (+ refrigeration) **makes** 32
Falafel can be made a day ahead; store, covered, in the refrigerator.

greek meatballs

1 tablespoon olive oil
1 onion, finely chopped
2 cloves garlic, crushed
1 pound lean ground lamb
1 egg
1½ cups stale breadcrumbs
2 tablespoons lemon juice
¼ cup finely chopped fresh flat-leaf parsley
¼ cup finely chopped fresh mint
⅓ cup all-purpose flour
olive oil, extra, for shallow-frying
yogurt (optional)

1 Heat oil in medium skillet, add onion and garlic; cook, stirring, until onion is softened. Cool.
2 Combine onion mixture with lamb, egg, breadcrumbs, juice, parsley and mint in large bowl. Cover, refrigerate 1 hour.
3 Roll level tablespoons of mixture into balls; toss balls in flour, shake away excess. Heat extra oil in large skillet; shallow-fry meatballs, in batches, until cooked through. Drain on paper towels.
4 Serve meatballs with yogurt, if desired.

prep + cook time 1 hour (+ refrigeration) **makes** 50
The oil should be very hot before cooking the meatballs. Ground beef can also be used in this recipe.

glossary

allspice also called pimento or jamaican pepper. Available whole or ground.

almonds

flaked paper-thin slices.

slivered thin lengthways-cut pieces.

artichoke, the bud of a large plant from the thistle family; has tough, petal-shaped leaves and an inedible prickly choke that should be discarded leaving the tender artichoke heart. Artichoke hearts are also available in brine in cans or in glass jars.

arugula also callet rocket, a bitter salad green with a peppery, mustard flavor. Baby arugula is milder.

beans

fava also called broad. Fresh and frozen forms should be peeled twice, discarding the outer long green pod and the tough beige-green inner shell.

white in this book, some recipes may simply call for 'white beans', a generic term used for cannellini, navy or great northern beans – all of which can be substituted for each other.

beets a firm, round root vegetable that may be either golden or deep red; golden beets are usually less sweet.

bread

brioche can be made in the shape of a loaf or roll. A rich, French yeast bread with a dark, golden, flaky crust; typically baked in a fluted pan.

ciabatta in italian, the word means 'slipper', which is the traditional shape of this white bread with a crisp crust.

pita a pocket bread sold in large, flat pieces that separate into two thin rounds. Also available in small thick pieces called pocket pita.

sourdough made by using a small amount of 'starter dough' (dough from a previous batch, containing a yeast culture). Part of the resulting dough is then saved to use as the starter dough next time.

Turkish; comes in long (about 18 inch) flat loaves as well as individual rounds. Made from wheat flour and sprinkled with sesame seeds.

breadcrumbs

packaged fine-textured, crunchy, purchased white breadcrumbs.

stale one- or two-day-old bread made into crumbs by blending or processing.

butter use salted or unsalted (sweet) butter; 8 tablespoons is equal to one stick (4 ounces).

calamari see squid.

caper berries fruit formed after the caper buds have flowered; caper berries are pickled, usually with stalks intact.

capers the gray-green buds of a warm climate (usually Mediterranean) shrub; sold dried and salted or pickled in a vinegar brine. Capers should be rinsed well before using.

cayenne pepper a long, thin-fleshed, very hot red chile usually sold dried and ground.

cheese

blue cheeses mottled with blue veining. Varieties include firm and crumbly stilton types to mild, creamy brie-like cheeses.

bocconcini baby mozzarella; walnut-sized, delicate, semi-soft, white cheese. Spoils rapidly so must be kept under refrigeration, in brine, for 2 days at most.

cream cheese also known as Philly or Philadelphia, a soft, cows-milk cheese.

feta a crumbly textured goat or sheep milk cheese with a sharp, salty taste.

goat made from goat milk; has an earthy, strong taste. Available as soft and firm, and in various shapes and sizes, sometimes rolled in ash or herbs.

haloumi a firm, cream-colored sheep-milk cheese matured in brine; can be grilled or fried, briefly, without breaking down. Should be eaten while still warm as it becomes tough and rubbery on cooling.

mascarpone a cultured cream product made similarly to yogurt. It's a buttery-rich,

cream-like cheese made from cows milk. Ivory-colored, soft and delicate, with the texture of softened butter.

mozzarella a soft, spun-curd cheese. It has a low melting point and elastic texture when heated; adds texture rather than flavor.

ricotta the name for this soft, white, cows-milk cheese roughly translates as 'cooked again'. It's made from whey, a by-product of other cheese-making, to which fresh milk and acid are added. Ricotta is a sweet, moist cheese with a slightly grainy texture.

romano a hard cheese with excellent keeping qualities. Made from sheep milk, this straw-colored cheese has a grainy texture and is mainly used for grating. Substitute with Parmesan.

Parmesan also known as Parmigiano; a hard, grainy, cow-milk cheese. The curd is salted in brine for a month before being aged for up to two years in humid conditions.

chervil herb with a mild fennel flavor.

chickpeas also called garbanzos, an irregularly round, sandy-colored legume.

chile

banana also known as wax chiles or hungarian peppers; are almost as mild as bell peppers but have a distinctively sweet sharpness to their taste. Sold in varying degrees of ripeness, they can be found in pale olive green, yellow and red varieties at most supermarkets.

flakes dried, deep-red, dehydrated chilli slices and whole seeds.

long red available both fresh and dried; a generic term used for any moderately hot, long (2½-3 inches), thin chile.

thai red also known as 'Thai bird chiles'; small, very hot and bright red in color.

chorizo a sausage of Spanish origin, made of coarsely ground pork and highly seasoned with garlic and chiles.

cilantro also known as chinese parsley; the bright-green leafy portion of the coriander plant, this herb has a pungent flavor. Stems and roots of cilantro may also be used; wash well before chopping. Coriander is also available ground or as seeds, but these are no substitute for fresh cilantro as the tastes are very different.

coppa a salted dried sausage made from the neck or shoulder of pork. Is deep red in color and is available both mild and spicy.

crème fraîche mature fermented cream having a slightly tangy, nutty flavor and velvety texture. Minimum fat content 35%.

eggplant purple-skinned vegetable that can also be purchased char-grilled, packed in oil, in jars. When buying fresh, choose smooth-skinned vegetable that's heavy for it's size.

fennel also known as anise; a white to very pale green-white, firm, crisp, roundish vegetable about 3-5 inches in diameter. The bulb has a slightly sweet flavor but the leaves (fronds) have a much stronger taste. Also the name given to dried seeds having a licorice flavor.

fish fillets, firm white any firm white boneless fish fillet – cod, flounder, sole, haddock and halibut are all good choices. Check for any small pieces of bone in fillets and use tweezers to remove them.

flour

plain an all-purpose flour made from wheat.

rice a fine flour made from ground white rice.

self-rising plain flour sifted with baking powder in the proportion of 1 cup flour to 2 teaspoons baking powder.

ghee also known as clarified butter; butter that has had its milk solids removed, so it can be heated to a high temperature without burning.

grape leaves cryovac-packed leaves in brine can be found in Middle-Eastern food shops and some delicatessens; these must be rinsed well and dried before using. Vine leaves in brine are also available in jars and packets from supermarkets.

harissa a Moroccan sauce or paste made from dried chiles, cumin, garlic, oil and caraway seeds. Is available from Middle-Eastern food stores.

lettuce, baby romaine the traditional caesar salad lettuce. Long, with leaves ranging from dark green on the outside to almost white near the core; the leaves have a stiff center rib that gives a slight cupping effect to the leaf.

mussels buy from a fish market where there is reliably fresh fish; must be tightly closed when bought, indicating they are alive. Before cooking, scrub the shells with a strong brush and remove the beards; discard any shells that do not open after cooking.

mustard, wholegrain also called seeded. A French-style coarse-grain mustard made from crushed mustard seeds and Dijon-style french mustard.

octopus a member of the mollusk family, octopus have a rich, flavorful meat popular in the Meditteranean. Frozen octopus is already precleaned of the inedible eyes and beak, it is available from fish markets, Asian and Latin grocery stores, as well as some gourmet grocery stores.

oil

cooking spray use a cholesterol-free cooking spray made from canola oil. Alternatively, use a refillable spray canister.

olive made from ripened olives. Extra virgin and virgin are the best, while extra light or light refers to taste not fat levels.

vegetable from plants rather than animal fats.

olives

anchovy-stuffed green manzanilla medium-sized green or black pickled olives; found at gourmet grocery stores.

green those harvested before fully ripened and are, as a rule, denser and more bitter than their black relatives.

kalamata small, sharp-tasting, brine-cured black olives.

ligurian very small black olives with a nutty flavor.

niçoise small black olives.

pimiento-stuffed green a green olive with a lively, briny bitterness and stuffed with a morsel of bell pepper, which adds color.

Sicilian dark olive green in color; can be found almost everywhere olives are sold. Brine-cured Sicilian olives are smooth and fine-skinned, crisp and crunchy to the bite – they have a refreshingly piquant, buttery flavor.

onion

scallion or, incorrectly, shallot; an immature onion picked before the bulb has formed, having a long, green edible stalk.

red also known as Spanish, red Spanish or bermuda onion; a sweet-flavored, large, purple-red onion.

shallots also called french shallots, golden shallots or eschalots; small, brown-skinned, elongated members of the onion family. Grows in tight clusters similar to garlic.

spring onions with small white bulbs and long narrow, green leafy tops.

pancetta pork belly that is cured but not smoked; bacon can be substituted.

paprika ground dried sweet red bell pepper; there are many types available, including sweet, hot, mild and smoked.

peppercorns, black picked when the berry is not quite ripe, then dried until it shrivels and the skin turns dark brown to black. Strongly flavored.

phyllo also known as fillo. A tissue-thin pastry dough typically sold frozen, in sheets, that is available at most grocery stores. Frozen phyllo can be stored for up to a year. Simply refrigerate overnight to thaw. Do not refreeze.

pine nuts also known as pignoli; not, in fact, a nut but a small, cream-colored kernel from pine cones. To toast, place in a small, dry skillet over medium-high heat. Shake skillet frequently and toast until fragrant.

pistachio pale green, delicately flavored nut inside hard off-white shells. To peel, soak shelled nuts in boiling water for about 5 minutes; drain, pat dry with paper towels. Rub skins with a cloth to peel.

polenta also known as cornmeal; a flour-like cereal made of dried corn (maize). Also the name of the dish made from it.

pomegranate molasses is thicker, browner and more concentrated than grenadine, the sweet, red pomegranate syrup used in cocktails. Has a tart, fruity quality similar to balsamic vinegar. It is available from Middle-Eastern food stores, and gourmet grocery stores.

prosciutto cured, air-dried, pressed ham. Usually sold thinly sliced.

quail small, delicately flavored, domestically grown game birds ranging in weight from ½-¾ pound; also known as partridge.

quince yellow-skinned fruit with a hard texture and an astringent, tart taste; eaten cooked or as a preserve.

radish a peppery root vegetable related to the mustard plant. The small round red variety is the mildest.

rice

arborio small, round-grain rice, well-suited to absorb a large amount of liquid; especially suitable for risottos.

long-grain elongated grain, remains separate when cooked; most popular steaming rice in South-East Asia.

medium-grain previously sold as Calrose rice; versatile rice that can be substituted for short- or long-grain rice if necessary.

short-grain a fat, almost round-grain rice with a high starch content; tends to clump together when cooked.

rosewater called gulab in India. An extract made from crushed rose petals; used for its aromatic quality. Available from Middle-Eastern food stores and some delicatessens.

saffron available in strands or ground form;

imparts a yellow-orange color to food once infused. Quality varies greatly; the best is the most expensive spice in the world. Should be stored in the freezer.

sashimi skinless, boneless raw fish pieces certified as safe to eat. Use the freshest, sashimi-quality fish you can find. Raw fish sold as sashimi has to meet stringent guidelines regarding its handling and treatment after leaving the water. We suggest you seek local advice from authorities before eating any raw seafood.

scallops a bivalve mollusk with a fluted shell valve.

sesame seeds black and white are the most common of this small oval seed, but there are red and brown varieties also.

sopressa a semi-hard pork salami typically flavored with pepper, cloves, cinnamon, nutmeg, rosemary and garlic; hot or mild.

squid also called calamari. Precleaned squid hoods can be purchased frozen either whole or already sliced into rings. Cooking time should always be short as squid becomes rubbery when overcooked.

sterilizing jars place cleaned glass jars on their sides in a large saucepan; cover with cold water. Cover pan, bring to the boil, and boil for 20 minutes. Carefully remove jars from water; drain. Stand jars, top-side up, on a wooden board. The heat from the jars will cause any remaining water to evaporate quickly. Place jars, on baking sheets, in a cold oven (do not allow the jars to touch); heat oven temperature to 250°F (225°F convection), then leave jars in oven 30 minutes. Plastic screw-top lids give a good seal (plastic snap-on lids are not airtight enough). Plastic lids must be well washed, rinsed and dried, or put through the dishwasher.

sugar

brown an extremely soft, finely granulated sugar retaining molasses for its characteristic color and flavor.

toasting nuts place in a small dry skillet over medium-high heat. Shake skillet frequently and toast until fragrant. For large quantities, place on rimmed baking sheet and bake 350°F (325°F convection), stirring frequently, until golden.

veal scallop a thin slice of meat that requires only a very quick cooking time.

vinegar

balsamic made from trebbiano grapes; it is a deep rich brown color with a sweet and sour flavor.

cider (apple cider) made from crushed fermented apples.

red wine based on fermented red wine.

sherry made from a blend of wines and left in wood vats to mature, where they develop a rich mellow flavor.

white made from cane sugar.

white wine made from white wine.

watercress one of the cress family, a large group of peppery greens. Highly perishable, so must be used as soon as possible after purchase.

endive also known as belgian endive; its cigar-shaped, tightly packed heads have pale, yellow-green tips, and a delicately bitter flavor. Eaten cooked or raw.

yeast a ¼ ounce package of active dry yeast (2 teaspoons) is equal to ½ ounce compressed yeast; they can be substituted for each other.

yogurt use plain, unflavored yogurt, unless otherwise specified.

zest the colorful, aromatic outer layer of citrus fruit that adds flavor to a dish. For best results use a microplane grater or vegetable peeler and avoid the bitter white pith layer beneath the zest.

zucchini also called courgette; harvested when young, its edible flowers can be stuffed then deep-fried or oven-baked.

index